On Business And For Pleasure

A Self-Study Workbook

For Advanced Business English Students

First published by O Books, 2010

O Books is an imprint of John Hunt Publishing Ltd., The Bothy, Deershot Lodge, Park Lane, Ropley,
Hants, SO24 0BE, UK
office1@o-books.net
www.o-books.net

Distribution in:

UK and Europe
Orca Book Services
orders@orcabookservices.co.uk
Tel: 01202 665432 Fax: 01202 666219
Int. code (44)

USA and Canada
NBN
custserv@nbnbooks.com
Tel: 1 800 462 6420 Fax: 1 800 338 4550

Australia and New Zealand
Brumby Books
sales@brumbybooks.com.au
Tel: 61 3 9761 5535 Fax: 61 3 9761 7095

Far East (offices in Singapore, Thailand,
Hong Kong, Taiwan)
Pansing Distribution Pte Ltd
kemal@pansing.com
Tel: 65 6319 9939 Fax: 65 6462 5761

South Africa
Stephan Phillips (pty) Ltd
Email: orders@stephanphillips.com
Tel: 27 21 4489839 Telefax: 27 21 4479879

Text copyright Michael Berman 2009

Design: Stuart Davies

ISBN: 978 1 84694 304 1

A CIP catalogue record for this book is available
from the British Library.

Printed by Digital Book Print

O Books operates a distinctive and ethical publishing philosophy in
all areas of its business, from its global network of authors to
production and worldwide distribution.

On Business And For Pleasure

A Self-Study Workbook

For Advanced Business English Students

Michael Berman

BOOKS

Winchester, UK
Washington, USA

CONTENTS

Introduction

The workbook is called *On Business & for Pleasure* because although it has been designed to help you with your work, it is hoped that the challenges it sets will, at the same time, prove to be enjoyable. An Answer Key has been included so you can check what you have done, and thus work independently, if that is what suits you best. And the exercises are of the kind of length that will enable you to work on them when you have relatively short periods of time to spare, such as while commuting to and from work on public transport. The size of the book should make this convenient too, with it being available in paperback size rather than in a larger format.

You will probably find that working through the material on a regular basis will be of more value than an initial burst of enthusiasm followed by a long lapse. In other words, doing a little on a regular basis is what is recommended rather than attempting to complete everything all in one go, with it going "in one ear and out of the other" so to speak.

Having studied a subject for a very long time, there is a danger of falling into the trap of thinking we know everything there is to know about it. However, there is always more to learn, especially in the case of a living language that is changing all the time. Hopefully, this workbook will go some way towards showing this to be the case.

Working through the material with a good English-English dictionary is to be recommended, ideally one that has been specifically produced for students of English as a Foreign Language, such as the Longmans Dictionary of Contemporary English or the Advanced Learners Dictionary published by Oxford University Press.

Visualizing your Ideal Job

Choose the best answer from each pair of alternatives. In most cases, only one of the answers is correct, but sometimes they both might be suitable. So be careful!

How much time do you spend 1 <u>bitching / to bitch</u> about your lousy boss, ridiculously low salary, hellish commute 2 <u>and etc. / and so on</u>? As satisfying 3 <u>as / than</u> a good gripe session is, you're 4 <u>losing / wasting</u> precious energy 5 <u>in / on</u> the wrong picture. Five minutes a day spent 6 <u>to visualize / visualizing</u> your 7 <u>ideal / idealistic</u> work-life and fashioning a plan to get you there will move you 8 <u>far / much</u> 9 <u>closer / nearer</u> to your goal than 30 minutes of moaning and groaning 10 <u>about / at</u> what you don't want. The most successful entrepreneurs love what 11 <u>do they do / they do</u>. So if you haven't quite 12 <u>figured / worked</u> out where your passion 13 <u>lays / lies,</u> start 14 <u>paying / to pay</u> attention instead 15 <u>of / to</u> what it is that does hold your interest. In 16 <u>other / the other</u> words, try to 17 <u>tune / tuning</u> into what it is you really love and want to do. What characteristics or talents do people compliment you 18 <u>for / on</u>? What kind of work or lifestyles do you envy? And if you don't 19 <u>still / yet</u> have the knowledge or skills to turn your heart work 20 <u>into / on</u> a business venture, 21 <u>do / make</u> it your business to fill the gaps. Remember that unless you 22 <u>don't walk / walk</u> out into the unknown, the 23 <u>chances / odds</u> of making a profound difference in your life are 24 <u>minimal / minimum</u>. But to 25 <u>avoid / prevent</u> yourself from being overwhelmed - yet still make headway - break your larger goal down into more manageable steps. And at the same 26 <u>moment / time</u> you're setting your 27 <u>sights / vision</u> on achieving your future goal, be 28 <u>aware / mindful</u> of how much abundance you have in your life right now! Changing course is a journey. 29 <u>Add up / Count</u> your blessings and enjoy the 30 <u>ride / trip</u>. When you think about it, it's all we really have.

Verbs with Dependent Prepositions

Match the numbers on the left with the letters on the right to complete the sentences, like the example.

Example: **2-g**

1. Some people insist
2. **Don't delude yourself**
3. You can stop yourself
4. Instead of living with my parents, we're looking forward
5. There is no magic formula. The only way you'll succeed
6. As you clearly have difficulty
7. The sales staff can be extremely persuasive so make sure you don't let them talk you
8. If you're tired
9. One way to reduce the cost of your bills is to get into the habit
10. You can't criticize me
11. I know you warned me
12. Instead of accusing me
13. Instead of complaining

a. about never having any money, why don't you do something about it?
b. against buying a new car but I'm afraid I just couldn't resist the temptation.
c. for overspending because you're just as guilty of it as I am.
d. from making silly purchases of things you rarely or never use if you try before you buy.
e. in making ends meet, you should perhaps consider taking on some extra work.
f. in reducing your overdraft is by spending less.

g. **into believing that a want is a need because it is a recipe for financial disaster.**

h. into buying something you don't really need.

i. of being lazy, why don't you go out to work?

j. of never having any money, you need to do something about it.

k. of shopping around.

l. on buying the biggest and the best, no matter what the cost.

m. to being able to save up enough money to have a home of our own one day.

Crossword Puzzles

Answer the clues across to complete the grids:

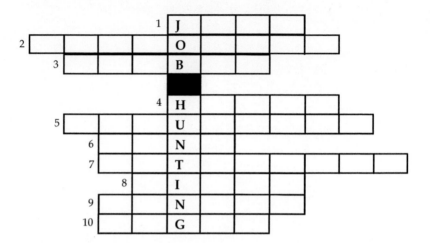

1. All work and no play makes ..... a dull boy
2. At the moment all I have is a ..... job but I'm looking for something permanent.
3. If you're ..... to work due to long-term illness, you can receive incapacity benefit.
4. Many ..... make light work
5. to lay someone off means to make someone .....
6. If you're so unhappy in your job, why don't you hand in your .....?
7. If you have the right qualifications, you'll be invited for an .....
8. The abbreviation CV stands for curriculum .....
9. to work your ..... to the bone
10. I ..... to inform you that your application was unsuccessful.

***

1. to take a risk with money
2. Money is the ..... of all evil.
3. If you want a clear conscience, you should ..... your money in an ethical bank.
4. If you're in ....., you'll need to take out a loan.
5. All work and no ..... makes Jack a dull boy.
6. The .. wage is the lowest amount of money an employer is allowed to pay you an hour.
7. I hope you don't mind my asking, but how much do you ..... a week?
8. If you want to buy a house or a flat, you can take out a ......
9. Money doesn't grow on ......
10. what you pay for professional services
11. The bank manager told me I had to reduce my ......
12. When the bank is closed, you can withdraw money from a ....machine.

Looking for a Job? - Get a Head Start

Choose the best answer from each pair of alternatives. In most cases, only one of the answers is correct, but sometimes they both might be suitable. So be careful!

Your 1 <u>curriculum vitae / resumé</u> is 2 <u>a / the</u> single most important weapon in your armoury when it comes to job 3 <u>hunting / searching</u>. A prospective 4 <u>chief / employer</u> will often 5 <u>make a snap judgment / reach a verdict</u> the 6 <u>moment / second</u> they read it and even the most qualified people on the planet can find themselves rejected if the submission fails to come up 7 <u>to / with</u> scratch. So how can you give yours the 8 <u>advantage / edge</u>? 9 <u>A/ The</u> secret is to 10 <u>avoid / prevent</u> making it too fancy and complicated because if it is too clever and unreadable it will 11 <u>more than likely / probably</u> go straight in the 12 <u>bin / out tray</u>. Don't try 13 <u>making / to make</u> jokes and never slag off previous employers. And never try 14 <u>smudging / to smudge</u> dates and jobs to hide periods of unemployment. The most basic of checks will expose your deceit and ruin any chance 15 <u>of getting / to get</u> the job.

16 <u>Set off / Start off</u> with your name, address and contact details clearly listed 17 <u>at / in</u> the top of the page. Follow this with a profile of yourself 18 <u>that / which</u> should include 19 <u>a lay-out / an outline</u> of your skills, 20 <u>experience / experiences</u> and immediate career goals. After this you can put in your career history - in reverse chronological order - with brief descriptions of your responsibilities and achievements. Then comes education, interests and references.

The odd one out (i)

Use each clue to connect two of the words below (underline them). You will then discover one word which is not in a pair!

For example:

Extra money paid to public employees in London to cover the higher cost of living in the capital

weighting allowance

1. The lowest amount an employer can pay an hour
2. A welcome surprise!
3. Paid by the State to people who have been too ill to work for at least 28 weeks
4. regular salary increase you receive each year
5. You receive this from your company if you're laid off
6. In some companies this takes the form of a thirteenth salary
7. Paid by the State to unemployed people who are available for and actively looking for work
8. Paid by the State to people between 16 and 60 who are on a low income who are not in full-time paid work
9. Extras on top of your salary, such as free meals or uniforms
10. This shows your employer how much to deduct from your salary each month

allowance / annual / benefit / benefits / bonus / Christmas / code / council / fringe / incapacity / income/ increment / jobseekers / minimum / pay / rebate / redundancy / support / tax / tax / wage/

The odd word is _____

Job-Hunting

Choose the most appropriate answer from each pair of alternatives. But be careful because sometimes both choices may be correct!

1) If / When you're looking for 2) a job / work, the 3) more / most important thing is to be determined. So even 4) if / though you're rejected, you must refuse to be deterred and keep on 5) to try / trying for that way you'll succeed 6) at / in the end. And there's no point 7) in feeling / to feel sorry 8) about / for yourself as you'll achieve 9) absolutely / totally nothing that way. In my own case, for example, I remember 10) receiving / to receive countless "regret to inform you" letters in the post before I eventually found what I was after 11) despite / in spite my qualifications. 12) However / Moreover, regardless of all the 13) drawbacks / setbacks I had along the 14) path / way, I never once gave up. I can 15) assure / ensure you that there is a job out there waiting for you and all you need to do is to be patient. I'm 16) in no doubt / without a doubt that 17) at / by this time next year all your 18) problems / troubles will be behind you and you'll be in regular full-time employment again so please stop 19) to worry / worrying. And even 20) if / though you don't manage to find a job, it's not 21) an / the end of the world so try 22) getting / to get things in 23) perspective / prospectus. For, 24) at / by the end of the day, 25) as long as / so long as you, and those you love, are in good health, nothing else really matters that much.

Writing a Covering Letter for a Job Application

From each set of alternatives, select the most appropriate choice of wording. Sometimes more than one option might be acceptable, and sometimes perhaps none of them will be:

1.
a. The name, address, and phone number of the person you are writing to on the left hand side of the page.
b. Your name, address, and phone number on the left hand side of the page.
c. The name, address, and phone number of the person you are writing to on the left hand side of the page, followed by your name, address, and phone number.
d. Your name, address, and phone number on the left hand side of the page, followed by the name, address, and phone number of the person you are writing to.
e. Leave this section blank as your details are on your CV and the person you are writing to knows his or her details in any case.

2.
a. Date
b. No date required as it will be on the postmark

3.
a. Dear Mr. _____., Mrs. _____, or Ms. _____,
b. Hello!
c. How are you?
d. The solution to all your problems!

4.
a. I am writing to apply for the English teaching position advertised in the *Camden Times*.

b. I am writing to apply for the position of English teacher advertised in the *Camden Times*.

c. I am applying for the post of English teacher that was advertised in the *Camden Times*

d. This is a letter of application for the job of English teacher advertised in the *Camden Times*.

e. I want to apply for the English teacher position advertised in the *Camden Times*.

f. I am writing to apply for the English teacher profession. I saw it advertised in the *Camden Times*.

5.

a. As requested, I am enclosing a completed job application, my certification, my resumé and three references.

b. As requested, I am enclosing a completed job application, my certification, my CV and three references.

c. As requested, I am enclosing a completed job application, my certification, my CV and three referees.

d. As requested, I am enclosing a completed job application, my certification, my resumé and three referees.

e. Everything you requested is enclosed.

6.

a. The opportunity presented in this listing is very interesting, and I believe that my considerable experience and qualifications will make me a very competitive candidate for this position.

b. The possibility presented in this listing is very interesting, and I know that my considerable experience and qualifications will make me a very competitive candidate for this position.

c. The opportunity presented in this advertisement sounds very interesting, and I believe that my considerable experience and qualifications will make me a very competitive candidate for this position.

d. The possibility presented in this advertisement is just what I'm looking for, and I know that my considerable experience and qualifications will make me a very competitive candidate for this position.

e. I'd love to get my teeth into a job like this and I know I'm just the person you've been looking for.

7.

a. The key strengths that I possess for success in this position include reliability, commitment, and strong interpersonal skills, all of which should stand me in good stead in view of the nature of the job.

b. The key strengths that I possess include reliability, commitment, and strong interpersonal skills, all of which should stand me in good stead in view of the nature of the job.

c. The key strengths that I possess and that I believe would make me a suitable candidate include reliability, commitment, and strong interpersonal skills, and that's why you should give me the job.

d. I would say that my strong points include reliability, total commitment, and strong interpersonal skills.

e. People tell me that my good points include my reliability, commitment, and my strong interpersonal skills, and I promise I won't let you down.

f. The key strengths that I believe would make me a suitable candidate include reliability, commitment, and strong interpersonal skills, all of which should stand me in good stead in view of the nature of the job.

8.

a. Please see my resumé for additional information on my

experience.

b. Please see my CV for additional information on my experience.

c. For additional information on my experience, please see my resumé.

d. For additional information on my experience, please see my CV.

e. For additional information on my experience, all you need to do is ask.

9.

a. Thank you for your time and consideration. I look forward to speaking with you about this employment opportunity.

b. Thank you for your time and consideration, and I look forward to convincing you of my suitability when you invite me for an interview.

c. Thank you for your time and consideration, and I know you won't regret choosing me.

d. Thank you for your time and consideration, and I hope you will give me the opportunity to show you what I can do by inviting me for an interview.

e. As the job is surely as good as mine already, all I need to know is when you'd like me to start!

f. By the way, how many sick days a year would I be entitled to if I got the job?

10.

a. Sincerely,

b. Yours sincerely,

c. Faithfully,

d. Yours faithfully,

e. Your obedient servant,

f. With all good wishes,

Uncountable Nouns

Fill each of the gaps in these sentences with a suitable uncountable noun:

1. To be honest with you, when I heard my boss was finally going to retire after all these years, it was ..... to my ears!

2. We are not prepared to take any risks at all because the ..... and well-being of our staff is, and always will be, our primary concern.

3. They say no ..... is good ..... but I'm not sure how true that is.

4. ..... doesn't grow on trees you know, which is why we must spend what we do have wisely.

5. Now that the rate of ..... is so high, it's not so easy to find a job as it used to be.

6. The next time you place an order for ....., don't forget to added headed paper to the list. But you needn't order any more envelopes as we still have plenty left from the last time.

7. Although we have clearly made some ..... over the last year, we still have some way to yet before we can say we are definitely out of the woods and back on an even keel again.

8. The office was hardly impressive and the only ..... to be seen in the room was a rickety chair and a desk.

9. There is a considerable amount of ..... to suggest that missing breakfast in the morning adversely affects one's efficiency at work.

10. The only ..... I'll need for my presentation is an Overhead Projector and a flipchart.

11. According to the ..... on this candidate's CV, she already has considerable experience in this field and thus, on paper at least, she seem to be just what we're looking for.

12. In order to increase output, we clearly need to invest in new ..... for the factory. Compared to our competitors, what we have at the moment is antiquated and belongs in a museum!

13. Unfortunately the negative press we had had recently has done the company a lot of ..... and it will take some considerable time to recover from it.

14. The suggestions for improving business that you have come up with have given me plenty of ..... for thought.

15. If you are in need of legal ....., the best thing to do would be to consult a lawyer.

16. The market ..... we have carried out suggests that there is likely to be a great demand for the product so the future looks promising.

17. I've got so much ..... to do these days that I'm seriously considering employing a secretary.

18. I get so much ..... in my inbox these days that most of it I delete without even bothering to read it.

Plural Nouns

Fill each of the gaps in these sentences with a suitable plural noun:

1. I made the mistake of investing all my ..... in the venture so now that it's failed I'm in a big mess.
2. Please keep all your personal ..... with you at all times when travelling on London Underground.
3. Office space on the ..... of London, not surprisingly, tends to be a lot cheaper than in the centre.
4. The ..... you ordered were delivered to the wrong address, which is why you never received them.
5. The ..... on you getting the job are unfortunately extremely low and you have to be prepared to be disappointed.
6. The ..... at the board meeting were taken by the company secretary.
7. I lost my job and I can't keep up with my mortgage repayments. In short, I'm in dire ..... so any help you can give me would be very much appreciated.
8. Although there is plenty of office space, the ..... are far from ideal so I think we'd better look for another location.
9. The ..... in the department store were right down this week - probably due to the tube strike.
10. You need to check through the Table of .....before I print it to make sure I haven't left anything out.
11. It's abundantly clear who wears the ..... in your household. If you hope to get your own way, you really need to be more assertive
12. I wonder what the lucky person who correctly selected the six numbers that were drawn in this Saturday's National Lottery is going to do with his .....?
13. It's a country where the rich are incredibly rich but where

the ... have absolutely nothing.

14. I heard you got the promotion you were after so I believe
..... are in order.

15. I'm afraid we have ways and ..... of making you relocate
even if you don't want to.

16. The ..... you are wearing really aren't appropriate I'm
afraid. You're expected to wear a suit and tie here.

17. How many ..... do you have? And are they still at school
or have they grown up and left home already?

Putting in for a Rise

When was the last time you put in for a rise at work, what reasons for the request did you present your boss with, and what was the result? Now read through the following passage and fill in the gaps with the correct answers. Then see if you can find suitable synonyms for all the phrasal verbs and, if working with a teacher, make sentences of your own with them for homework:

My boss was extremely put out when I put in for a rise even though I felt I'd put across my reasons in a convincing way and that had made out a strong case for myself. 1) ... He said that due to the current economic climate he wanted to put my request on hold for the moment but I told him that just wasn't good enough. 2) ... But I felt he was putting me down and I wasn't amused. I can only put down his reluctance to agree to the fact that he just does not value me and I'm just not prepared to put up with the situation any longer. 3) ... So I've decided to take up the offer of an interview for a new job in Manchester where a cousin of mine lives and he's offered to put me up for the night. 4) ... However, I won't put on any airs or graces and they'll just have to take me as they find me. 5) ..... Then, when I was eventually put through to the right department and they told me how much it would cost, it turned out to be so expensive that I decided to go by coach instead. I've also been thinking about starting my own company but I don't think I could put up the necessary capital and the risks involved put me off the idea. I'd be more than prepared to put in the necessary work but the fact that I'd have to submit a detailed business plan and apply for a substantial bank loan rather puts me off the idea.

a.   He then put forward a number of reasons for not agreeing to my request.
b.   However, walking out now would be putting the cart

17

before the horse because first I need to find somewhere else to go.

c. I explained how I could barely make ends meet on my present salary and that I was unable to put by anything for the future.

d. I phoned the station to find out about train times and the cost of the fare but I was put through to the wrong department.

e. I'll put on a smart suit and tie for the occasion because it could make all the difference.

Money Makes the World Go Round (i)

Match the descriptions on the left with the money expressions on the right:

1. a loan to house buyers
2. you might pay this if you lost a court case
3. paid for finding your neighbour's missing cat
4. government help for industry
5. what some students get to help pay for their studies
6. a property tax paid to your local council
7. something extra at Christmas maybe
8. a minus amount in your bank account
9. the type of money used by a country
10. hotel bills etc. paid by your company
11. the total amount of money you get, from all sources
12. extras paid on top of your salary e.g. free meals or a company car
13. paid to some top executives who are made redundant
14. earned by many salespeople instead of a salary

a. council tax
b. a mortgage
c. income
d. compensation / damages
e. commission
f. a grant
g. a subsidy
h. currency
i. a bonus
j. an overdraft
k. a golden handshake
l. a reward
m. expenses
n. perks / fringe benefits

Money Makes the World Go Round (ii)

Match the descriptions on the left with the money expressions on the right:

1. paid to you monthly
2. money paid to the government out of your earnings
3. what you pay to travel on a bus or train, or in a taxi
4. paid after you retire
5. indirect tax payable on services and goods in shops
6. you pay this to your landlord / landlady
7. paid to unemployed people
8. payment for professional services
9. money you earn in a deposit account
10. earned by waiters, porters, and taxi drivers
11. paid to you weekly
12. what you pay for committing an offence

a. rent
b. a wage
c. interest
d. a salary
e. a fee
f. a fare
g. tips
h. a pension
i. income tax
j. a fine
k. Value Added Tax
l. social security / unemployment benefit

Uncountable Nouns: How to refer to them (i)

A CAUSE OF is frequently used with uncountable nouns that designate something undesirable - UNEMPLOYMENT, for example.

A SUPPLY OF is frequently used with uncountable nouns that designate something that is needed - WATER, for example.

Sort the following uncountable nouns into two groups according to whether they can be used with A CAUSE OF or A SUPPLY OF, then practise using them by filling the gaps in the sentences:

anxiety / cash / distress / electricity / energy / equipment / food / gas / global warming / hardship / inflation / information / medicine / misery / poverty / trouble / misunderstanding / money / homelessness / stationery

1. We seem to have run out of headed notepaper and envelopes and need to order a new supply of .....
2. I hope I didn't give you any cause for ..... because of the way I behaved. If I did, I can assure you it wasn't intentional. The last thing I want to do is to upset you in any way.
3. Security of supply of ..... is key element for the functionality of the modern societies. For without everything would grind to a standstill.
4. Where do you get your supply of ..... from? You must have friends in very high places.
5. Cultural differences can be a cause of ..... in business negotiations, just as they can be in personal relationships.
6. The supply of all sorts of ..... over the internet without the need for a prescription is a real cause of concern to doctors.

7. One of the underlying causes of ..... is the level of monetary demand in the economy - how much money is being spent.

8. Having an ample supply of clean ..... is a top priority in an emergency. A normal active person needs to drink at least two quarts of water each day. Hot environments can double that amount.

The Value of Savings

Choose the best answer from each pair of alternatives. In most cases, only one of the answers is correct, but sometimes they both might be suitable. So be careful!

Sometimes I think it's 1) no/not worth 2) of trying / trying 3) building /to build up my savings because 4) who does know / who knows what tomorrow may bring or what 5) lays /lies around the next 6) bend / corner.

After all, what's the 7) point / use of putting money 8) away / by for our retirement when it's possible we might never even reach 9) so / such a 10) mature / ripe old age? Surely it would be better to enjoy 11) spending / to spend 12) it / them while we still can. The alternative would be to leave all your money in your 13) testament / will to your children. 14) However, / Moreover, 15) a / the truth is that it might be better for them if they learnt how to be independent instead, for if we 16) cover / wrap them up in cotton wool, they will never be able to manage without us.

Another 17) fact / factor to take into 18) account / consideration is that 19) at / in times of recession, interest 20) rates / ratios are so low in any case that investing in banks or building societies becomes pointless.

Uncountable Nouns: How to refer to them (ii)

A MEANS OF enables you to do something – A MEANS OF TRANSPORT, for example, enables you to travel.

A SOURCE is frequently used with something you can tap into – A SOURCE OF PLEASURE, for example.

Sort the following uncountable nouns into two groups according to whether they can be used with A MEANS OF or A SOURCE OF, then practise using them by filling the gaps in the sentences:

amusement / birth control / comfort / communication / discipline / energy / enlightenment / excellence / government / identification / information / inspiration / joy / knowledge / pleasure / recruitment / revelation / satisfaction / self-assessment / supervision / support/ taxation / waste disposal

1. There are various means of ….. we can use including asking to see your passport or your driving licence.
2. You seem to have no visible means of ….. so I wonder how you manage to get by.
3. To counter global warming and to ensure the future survival of our planet, we need to find alternative and renewable sources of …..
4. You'll find that your local library is a great source of ….. about the area in which you live.
5. The contraceptive pill is a means of ….., as is the use of a condom.
6. Unfortunately the President is a despot and the country has no democratic means of ….. at all.
7. Using landfill sites and incineration are both means of …..that are currently in use.

8. Studying the bible has proved to be a source of ….. to me and has completely transformed my life.

9. The example you have set, of starting with nothing and ending up a millionaire by the age of thirty, has been a source of ….. for me and I hope to be able to follow in your footsteps.

10. Oxford and Cambridge Universities both have a reputation for being sources of ….. in education and will no doubt continue to maintain their status for many decades to come.

Stress at Work

Choose the most appropriate answer from each pair of alternatives. But be careful because sometimes both choices may be correct!

They 1) <u>say / tell</u> that all work and no 2) <u>game / play</u> makes Jack a dull boy and I have no 3) <u>doubt / uncertainty</u> that 4) <u>it / there</u> is a great deal of 5) <u>true / truth</u> in this. For if all you 6) <u>do / make</u> is work, it is more or less inevitable that your health will eventually suffer as a result and that 7) <u>it / there</u> is a 8) <u>cost / price</u> to be paid for 9) <u>such / such a</u> behaviour. 10) <u>All in all / After all,</u> no boss wants any member of their staff to drop dead with a heart attack. That is why it is so important for employers to 11) <u>assure / ensure</u> that their employees are getting enough 12) <u>exercise / exercises</u> by ideally providing them 13) <u>for / with</u> a gym or at least free membership to a local Health Club. And they will soon find such an investment, though 14) <u>somehow / somewhat</u> costly, pays 15) <u>dividends / profits</u> as a healthy 16) <u>body / figure</u> means a healthy 17) <u>brain / mind</u> and will result in 18) <u>fewer / less</u> working days being lost due to sickness. 19) <u>Furthermore / Nonetheless,</u> the staff will undoubtedly appreciate such 20) <u>anxiety / concern</u> for their well-being and will respond positively to it.

One Word, Three Uses (i)

Find one word only which can be used appropriately in all three sentences. Here is an example:

You've been overworking recently and you really need to ..... a break.

Perhaps the most sensible thing to do would be to ..... some time out to reconsider your position before you come to any decisions regarding your future.

There's been a great improvement in the company's figures and it is the sales team who should ..... most of the credit for it.

Answer: take.

Q1

How much would I have to raise to buy a ..... in the company?

You need to think twice before you act because your whole future could be at .....

I am so confident that the business will be a success that I am prepared to ..... my reputation on it.

Q2

If we sold it to our customers at ..... price, we would not make any profit.

How much would it ..... if I decided to self-publish the book?

I agree that success is important but not at the ..... of your health.

Q3

If you ..... in stocks and shares, you have to be prepared for ups and downs.

I need a quick decision. So have we got a ..... or not?

You're a difficult person to ..... with, aren't you? I never imagined the negotiations were going to be so tough.

Q4

It's a real ..... at the price and if I were you I'd buy it.

When we booked the holiday we didn't ..... on having to pay a fuel surcharge as well so it came as a bit of a shock.

I don't feel comfortable having to ..... and I prefer shopping when the prices are fixed.

Q5

I know what you think it's worth but what did the estate agent ..... the house at?

To bring out the best in your staff, you really need to show you ..... them more highly than you do.

How on earth can put a ..... on human life? Surely it's a complete impossibility.

The abbreviation VAT stands for ..... added tax.

Q6

It's a real bargain and it would even be cheap at twice the .....!

If you're not careful, you're going to ..... yourself right out of the market. You need to be more realistic.

The offer made was well under the asking ..... for the property so it still hasn't been sold yet.

Q7

What's this extra ..... for? I thought you said VAT was included.

Mrs Hopkins is in ..... so you had better do what she tells you to or else you will get into trouble.

How much did the builders ..... you for the repairs they carried out?

How stressed out are you?

1. How do you react when something upsets you or winds you up?
a. You think about it for a day or two.
b. You can't get it out of your head for a week or more.
c. Your thoughts quickly turn to other things.

2. How do you feel when you think about all the jobs you have to do during the day?
a. You usually feel you can cope well despite the pressures.
b. You feel wound up but expect to get through it.
c. You feel overwhelmed and think you'll never be able to do them.

3. How does your body feel on a typical day?
a. Tense across the neck and shoulders.
b. Relaxed. Your breathing is always easy and slow.
c. Very stiff in the neck and shoulders and you're prone to frequent headaches.

4. How do you react to the situations you find yourself in feel during the course of an average day?
a. You tend to lose your temper over unimportant things.
b. You get more irritated by things going wrong then you would like.
c. You cope calmly with life's usual setbacks.

5. What's your sleeping pattern like?
a. You have no problems sleeping.
b. You wake up frequently during the night and often feel tired the next day.
c. You get odd nights of bad sleep but can usually make up for them.

6. How do you react when you think of what other people expect from you in life?

a. You panic and feel inadequate.

b. You can keep a sense of perspective. You know there are lots of things you can't do, and that's fine.

c. You take their opinions seriously but you don't lose any sleep over them.

Business or Economy Class?

Choose the best answer from each pair of alternatives. In most cases, only one of the answers is correct, but sometimes they both might be suitable. So be careful!

It 1 <u>seems / would seem</u> to me that 2 <u>business travellers / the business travellers</u> 3 <u>are often / often are</u> taken advantage of by travel companies, and that business class 4 <u>fares / fees</u> are 5 <u>far / much</u> more expensive than they need to be. In 6 <u>practice / practise,</u> what is happening is that the airlines are 7 <u>doing / making</u> enormous profits on a service that is 8 <u>hardly any different to / almost identical to</u> 9 <u>that / those</u> you get as an 10 <u>economical / economy</u> class passenger. Is it really 11 worth <u>to pay / paying</u> up to twice or even 12 <u>three times / thrice</u> 13 <u>a / the</u> cost of a normal ticket for a slightly better meal or a bit more 14 <u>legroom / leg space</u>? Will it result 15 <u>in / of</u> 16 <u>you / your</u> 17 <u>getting / to get</u> to your final destination 18 <u>any quicker / any more quickly</u>? Of course 19 <u>it doesn't / not.</u> And if 20 <u>having / to have</u> a newspaper is important to you or complimentary alcoholic drinks, why not 21 <u>buy / to buy</u> 22 <u>it / them</u> before your departure and take them with you? On the other hand, if it is your company 23 <u>footing / paying</u> the bill rather than you, perhaps it doesn't matter that much. 24 <u>However / Moreover,</u> if the money comes out of your own pocket, then my 25 <u>advice / advise</u> to you would be to think twice before you pay extra to travel business class next time.

Writing a Formal Letter of Complaint

From each set of alternatives, select the most appropriate choice of wording for a formal letter of complaint. Sometimes more than one option might be acceptable, and sometimes perhaps none of them will be:

Dear sir / madam,

1.

a.   How are you doing?
b.   Hope you're well.
c.   I trust this letter finds you in good health.
d.   How's it going?
e.   I hope you're well and enjoying life.
f.   _____ (no greeting necessary)

2.

a.   The reason why I am writing is to let you know how dissatisfied I am with _____
b.   I am writing to say how concerned / upset I am about_____
c.   I am contacting you to express my disappointment with_____
d.   I'm really pissed off with_____
e.   I can't tell you how fed up I am with_____
f.   I'm sick and tired of_____
g.   I am writing to complain in the strongest possible terms_____
h.   I'm writing to complain as strongly as I can_____

3.

a.   I find this state of affairs totally unacceptable.
b.   This really isn't on.
c.   This is really not what I would expect from reputable company like yours.
d.   I really expected a lot more / better from a company with your reputation.
e.   Have you never heard of customer care?
f.   You must be mad to think I'll put up with this.

4.

a.   Unless you rectify the problem / resolve this issue,
     _____

b.   Unless you are prepared to make amends for the problems you have caused me_____
c.   Unless you are prepared to offer me some form of compensation for the inconvenience I have had,
     _____

d.   Unless you resolve this issue without any further delay,_____
e.   Unless you pay me off, _____

Either:

5.

a.   _____you'll wish you had never been born.
b.   _____I make sure you'll live to regret what you've done.
c.   _____I'll sue you for every penny you've got.
d.   _____the next letter you receive will be from my solicitor.

e. _____I'll do everything I can to destroy you.

f. _____I'll do everything in my power to make your life a total misery.

Or:

6.

a. I will really have no choice but to_____
b. you will leave me with no choice but to_____
c. I will have no alternative but to_____
d. I am afraid I will have to_____
e. you'll force me to_____

7.

a. You'd better reply to this or else!
b. Looking forward to hearing from you
c. I trust that you will give this matter your urgent attention.
d. Your obedient servant
e. I would be most grateful if you would look into this matter as soon as possible.

8.

a. Yours sincerely,
b. Yours faithfully,
c. Kind regards,
d. Wishing you all the best,
e. Best wishes,

Are you a good Traveller?

1. When do you get to the station if you have a train to catch?
    a. ten minutes early b. an hour beforehand c. thirty seconds before the train pulls out

2. What do you take with you for a weekend break?
    a. a toothbrush b. just a few essentials in a plastic bag c. a large suitcase with clothes to suit every occasion

3. In a foreign restaurant, what would you choose to eat?
    a. a tried and tested favourite b. something simple like an omelette and chips c. you're the kind of person who is prepared to try anything once

4. What would you do if your holiday resort turned out to be rather dull?
    a. concentrate on getting a good suntan and reading b. try to cut the holiday short c. rally everyone together and make your own entertainment

5. If you lost your passport, what would you do?
    a. report it to your embassy and the local police b. wait until the very last day of your holiday before you act c. you always keep your passport safe so it couldn't possibly happen to you

6. What do you do on holiday when the weather is really scorching?
    a. slap on the oil and sun yourself all day b. stay outside for no more than ten minutes and wear a hat c. wear protective cream and sunbathe for no more than an hour or so

7. What would you do if you were travelling to a country

where you didn't speak the language?
a. manage to make yourself understood by using sign language b. take a crash course before you go and come back fluent c. buy a phrase book and learn a few essential phrases

8. What insurance cover do you arrange before travelling abroad?
a. you cover yourself for everything you possibly can b. you take out a basic policy providing cover for health and luggage c. you don't bother

9. What are you like on planes?
a. you pass the time by telling everyone you meet your life story b. you enjoy the in-flight movie c. you spend the whole flight in the toilet praying

10. You know you tend to get travel sick. So what precautions do you take?
a. take pills for it b. suffer the way nature intended c. stay at home

11. What would you do if your luggage went missing at the airport?
a. go back every day to look for it b. camp at the airport and make a big stink about it c. report the loss to an official in person, then in writing.

12. What do you do for money when you go abroad?
a. you take cash with b. a little cash and the rest in travellers cheques c. use your credit card

13. You know the local booze is really strong. So what do you

do?

a. challenge the bartender to a drinking competition b. try a couple to test it for yourself c. avoid it and stick to something you know instead

14. You're involved in a passionate holiday romance. What happens at the end of your stay there?
a. you agree to marry the person b. you enjoy it while it lasts but do not even think about the future c. feel lovesick for a few weeks but then move on and forget all about it

15. How do you behave when you go abroad?
a. you do whatever you please regardless of local customs b. you try to fit in with the locals c. you hole up in a plush five star hotel and so have little, if anything, to do with the locals

16. How honest are you when you go through Customs?
a. you always keep within the limits b. you sometimes go over the limit but always declare it c. you try to get away with as much as you can

17. What instructions do you leave before you go away?
a. you leave explicit instructions about where you can be contacted b. you tell people where you are going to stay c. you escape in silence

18. How far ahead do you plan trips?
a. months in advance b. on the spur of the moment c. a few weeks before you want to go

19. How much do you drink and / or smoke on a long flight?
a. more than usual b. the same as usual c. less or not at all

20. What do you do if you have a few hours to spare before a connecting flight?
    a. wait in the airport b. travel into town and do some sightseeing c. have a boozy meal at a local hotel

Using Low Emission forms of Transport

Choose the best answer from each pair of alternatives. In most cases, only one of the answers is correct, but sometimes they both might be suitable. So be careful!

1 <u>A / The</u> way we choose to travel significantly 2 <u>affects / effects</u> our impact on 3 <u>climate change / the climate change</u>. It's unlikely to be practical for us to give up our cars and stop 4 <u>flying / to fly</u> 5 <u>all together / altogether,</u> but we can make a significant difference by thinking more carefully 6 <u>about / of</u> the choices we make and also by looking 7 <u>into / through</u> alternatives. For example, it is high time 8 <u>to ask / we asked</u> ourselves if we really need 9 <u>flying / to fly</u> of if we can in fact go 10 <u>by / via</u> train instead. And for those of us genuinely concerned about 11 <u>future / the future</u> of our planet, as of course we all ought 12 <u>be / to be,</u> by using 13 <u>public transport / the public transport</u> whenever possible we can 14 <u>avoid / prevent</u> the need to drive and, at the same time, significantly 15 <u>decrease / reduce</u> our 16 <u>impact / influence</u> on climate change. So before 17 <u>driving / to drive</u> we should always check to see 18 <u>if / whether</u> the 19 <u>journey / voyage</u> is perhaps possible 20 <u>another / the other</u> way. Something else we can consider doing is to take a 21 <u>holiday / vacation</u> 22 <u>closer / nearer</u> to home. By holidaying in the UK instead of 23 <u>abroad / overseas,</u> it is possible for each of us to save as much as 10% of our annual carbon emissions. Alternatively, 24 how about 24 <u>taking / to take</u> one long holiday 25 <u>instead of / rather than</u> two to halve the number of flights?

A Code of Ethics for Tourists

Find the missing prepositions:

a. Travel 1. ..... a spirit of humility and 2. ..... a genuine desire to learn more 3. ..... the people of your host country.
b. Be sensitively aware 4. ..... the feelings of other people, preventing what might be offensive behaviour 5. ..... your part. This applies very much 6. ..... photography.
c. Cultivate the habit 7. ..... listening and observing, rather than merely hearing and seeing.
d. Realize that often the people 8. ..... the country you visit have time concepts and thought patterns different 9 ..... your own; this does not make them inferior, only different.
e. Instead 10. ..... looking 11. ..... that "beach paradise", discover the enrichment of seeing a different way of life 12. ..... other eyes.
f. Acquaint yourself 13. ..... local customs –people will be happy to help you.
g. Instead of the Western practice 14. ..... knowing all the answers, cultivate the habit 15. ..... listening.
h. Remember that you are only one of the thousands of tourists visiting the country, so do not insist 16. ..... special privileges.
i. If you really want your experience to be a "home away 17. ..... home", it is foolish to waste money 18. ..... travelling.
j. When you are shopping, remember that the "bargain" you obtained was only possible because 19. ..... the low wages paid 20. ..... the maker.
k. Do not make promises to people in your host country unless you are certain you can carry them 21. ....
l. Spend some time reflecting 22. ..... your daily experiences 23. ..... an attempt to deepen your understanding. It has

been said that what enriches you may rob and violate others.

Noun Phrases with Dependent Prepositions (i)

Match the numbers on the left with the letters on the right to complete the sentences, like the example.

Example: **2-i**

1. There is no point
2. **If you had no intention**
3. I have no hesitation
4. You'll have to excuse me if I'm a bit slow at first but I have no experience
5. I have no objection
6. I suppose the reason why I enjoy my work so much is that I get a kick
7. As I have no family ties to keep me here, I have no qualms whatsoever
8. The reason why I have doubts
9. To tell you the truth, I'm in two minds
10. I have a vested interest
11. You clearly have a flair
12. I don't understand this preoccupation you have

a. about accepting the job as I was really hoping for something a bit better.
b. about offering you the job is that I'm not sure I can depend on you.
c. about working overseas as long as it is somewhere hot.
d. for learning languages and a special way with words so perhaps you should consider a career as a translator.
e. in recommending Ms Smith for the job as I am sure she will be a great asset to your company.
f. in seeing the company succeed because I bought a large number of shares in it.

g. in your applying for the job because we are looking for someone who has done the same kind of work before.

h. of doing this kind of work before.

i. **of offering me the job in any case, then I don't understand why you invited me for the interview. It's been a complete waste of time for both of us.**

j. out of all the overseas travel it entails.

k. to working overtime as long as I get paid for it.

l. with wanting to make money when there are so many more important things in life.

One Word, Three Uses (ii)

Find one word only which can be used appropriately in all three sentences. Here is an example:

You've been overworking recently and you really need to ..... a break.

Perhaps the most sensible thing to do would be to ..... some time out to reconsider your position before you come to any decisions regarding your future.

There's been a great improvement in the company's figures and it is sales team who should ..... most of the credit for it.

Answer: take.

Q1

Have you come here on ..... or for pleasure?

How much I earn each week is none of your .....

If I let you purchase the product at cost price, I would quickly go out of .....

Q2

I'm afraid we don't keep that particular brand in ..... but we can order it for you.

We need to take ..... of the situation before we come to any decisions about what to do next.

Things are changing so rapidly that it is becoming increasingly difficult to keep ..... of what is going on these days.

Q3

The situation in the country is now out of ..... and the police can no longer ensure your safety.

By not allowing anyone else to take decisions apart from yourself, it has to be said you are acting like some kind of .....

freak.

I can assure you that we are fully in ….. of the situation and that you have nothing at all to worry about.

Q4

If you work here you will have to change the way you dress as it is not ….. policy to allow anyone to wear jeans to work,

Instead of sending our staff to a language school we organize in-….. classes.

We can't agree to your proposals as they are not in the …..'s best interests.

Q5

By agreeing to invest your savings for a fixed number of years, you can earn higher …..

To be frank, your proposal is of absolutely no ….. to me as I have already made other plans.

In view of the current economic situation, financial analysts are predicting that the Bank of England will decide on a rise in ….. rates.

Q6

According to the terms of the ….., tenants are not allowed to sub-let the property so what you are doing is in fact illegal.

The doctors are hoping that by fitting the patient with a pacemaker, it will give him a new ….. of life.

You can buy property freehold or …..hold in the UK. The former usually applies to houses whereas the latter applies to flats and is usually for a period of 99 or 999 years.

Linking Words (i)

Match the numbers on the left with the letters on the right to complete the sentences, like the example.

Example: **2-c**

1. Even though we haven't always seen eye-to-eye with each other,
2. **Regarding your application,**
3. We're unable to take you on permanently due to a number of factors,
4. Despite your lack of experience,
5. No matter where I go,
6. Some of the workers on the farm are just seasonal
7. As well as having a problem with anger management,
8. So unless you're prepared to make more of an effort,
9. Not only does the new Office Manager lead by example,
10. Nobody has any right to talk to me in that manner
11. Unless business picks up,
12. Unfortunately there are problems with all the proposals,
13. Considering how high the rate of unemployment is,

a. but she's also extremely well-organised and I must say I'm really impressed.
b. I am genuinely delighted for you.
c. **I regret to inform you that you have been unsuccessful on this occasion.**
d. I'll have no choice but to ask you to leave.
e. no matter which one we decide to opt for.
f. no matter who they are.
g. not least of which is the problem of arranging a work permit for you.
h. the standard of your work leaves a lot to be desired too.

i. trouble seems to follow me all the time.

j. we'll probably have to close down this branch and you'll all find yourselves being made redundant I'm afraid.

k. whereas others are permanent and work there all year round.

l. you make up for it with your commitment.

m. you should think yourself lucky to have any kind of job.

The odd one out (ii)

Use each clue to connect two of the words below (underline them). You will then discover one word which is not in a pair!

For example:

A plastic alternative to money   **credit card**

1. A lot of account holders object to paying them and say they're too high!
2. You can take these on holiday with you instead of cash
3. You can take one of these out if you want to go on a special holiday, buy a car, or have a new kitchen fitted in your home
4. Someone who cares about what their savings are used for by their bank
5. You can draw out money from this 24 hours a day, 7 days a week
6. You can arrange to pay your regular bills this way – your gas or electricity bills, for example.
7. This lets the bank know how safe it is to lend money to you
8. If your house burns down, you'll be covered by this
9. You can earn more interest in this than in a current one
10. The extra you can withdraw from your account when you have nothing left in it

account / bank / cashpoint / charges / cheques / credit / debit / direct / ethical / home / insurance / investor / limit / loan / machine / mortgage / overdraft / personal / rating / savings / travellers /

The odd word is _____

Discrimination in the Workplace

Choose the best answer from each pair of alternatives. In most cases, only one of the answers is correct, but sometimes they both might be suitable. So be careful!

In its 1 <u>broadest / widest</u> terms 2 <u>discrimination / the discrimination</u> in the workplace is when an employer or their employee treats you less favourably 3 <u>as / than</u> anyone else, and it can 4 <u>manifest / show</u> itself into two main types – direct and indirect. 5 <u>Direct / The Direct</u> discrimination tends to cover straightforward actions where an employee is obviously being treated less favourably 6 <u>because of / on account of</u> their sex or race. For example, 7 <u>consider / take</u> the case of a woman 8 <u>that / who</u> obviously is more qualified than the other members of staff 9 <u>in / under</u> consideration, but who is turned 10 <u>down / over</u> for promotion because she happens to be pregnant. As for 11 <u>indirect / the indirect</u> discrimination, it is a 12 <u>more subtle / subtler</u> version where it is not always obvious when the discrimination takes place. An example of this would be when 13 <u>it / there</u> is an imposed requirement or condition, 14 <u>that / which</u> 15 <u>leads to / results in</u> discrimination against individuals 16 <u>on the grounds of / for reasons of</u> gender or race. For instance: Imposing an age requirement 17 <u>in / on</u> a job advert, or 18 <u>asking / to ask</u> for qualifications above the requirement for the post. 19 <u>As / Together</u> with all legislation, it is one thing to identify someone breaking the law but 20 <u>another / the other</u> when it comes to 21 <u>implement / implementing</u> the rules. The office is a close community, at least in 22 <u>conditions / terms</u> of people's distance from each other, and it is a place where it is easy to feel 23 <u>intimidated / intimidating</u>. But the only way to get 24 <u>disposed / rid</u> of bad 25 <u>practice / practise</u> is to highlight it when you see it.

Homophones

Homophones are pairs of words with the same pronunciation but with a different spelling and a different meaning.

Answer the clues below to find pairs of homophones:

1a. We'll have to ..... up all the pros and cons before we come to any decision.
1b. I know it seems to be an impossible task but we'll find a ..... somehow. After all, we have no choice.
2a. To do this kind of work, you need to have nerves of ......
2b. If you ..... from your own company, it's known as embezzlement.
3a. There's no need to worry because I'm sure everything will work out all ..... in the end. Somehow it always does.
3b. You need to ..... all the details of what happened on this complaints form please.
4a. Managing to pull off such an important deal would be an amazing ..... and one to be very proud of.
4b. I hope you won't get cold ..... at the last minute and that you'll remain resolute or else we'll have no chance.
5a. I need these extra problems like a ..... in my head – I have more than enough trouble on my hands as it is.
5b. On the ....., I agree with you but not on every single point.
6a. I'm not the kind of person who likes to be ..... down so I don't suppose I'll stay in this job very long..
6b. They say time and ..... wait for no man and that's why you've really got no time to lose.
7a. He arrived just when he said he would, right on .....
7b. There's a ..... of people waiting for the bank to open, stretching right round the block.
8a. As long as you're prepared to be patient, I'm sure you'll find what you're looking for in the end. All you need to

do is to remember that ..... there's a will there's a way.

8b. You don't need to ..... a uniform, just a suit and tie.

9a. As the sole ..... to her father's estate, she's set to inherit a fortune.

9b. I don't know what's going to happen. Everything's up in the ..... at the moment.

10a. Please don't make a ..... – you're embarrassing me.

10b. I seem to have mislaid the contract you gave me to sign. Have you ..... it anywhere?

Race, Sex and Marital Discrimination

Employees are protected from discrimination by legislation broadly falling within the following areas: Sex, Race, Pay, Marital, and Disability. Read through these notes and then add the missing prepositions:

The Sex Discrimination Act 1975 and the Race Relations Act 1976 protect men and women 1. ...... discrimination 2. ...... the grounds of sex, marital status, colour, race, nationality, ethnic or national origins. The law protects applicants and employees who may be contract, self-employed, or part-time workers. The employer is ultimately responsible 3. ...... the actions of their employees.

If any member of a staff discriminates 4. ...... another, then it is both the staff member and the company who will be liable 5. ...... not taking reasonable steps to prevent the discrimination.

Pay Discrimination

The Equal Pay Act 1970 makes it unlawful to discriminate 6. ...... men and women 7. ...... regards to pay and other terms of employment. A person is entitled 8. ...... equal treatment 9. ...... someone 10. ...... the opposite sex who is employed on work of the same or broadly similar nature, and on work 11. ...... equal value.

Disability Discrimination

12. ...... the Disability Discrimination Act 1995 employees are protected 13. ...... discrimination 14. ...... the grounds of their disability and employers should take preventative and reasonable measures, so that a disabled person is not placed 15. ...... a disadvantage.

Conditionals

0   If you want to get to the top, you need to be more deter-
     mined.
1   If you want to get to the top, you'll need to be more deter-
     mined.
2   If you wanted to get to the top, you'd need to be more
     determined.
3   If you had wanted to get to the top, you'd have needed to
     be more determined.

The zero conditional is used to express general truths, the first
conditional is used to talk about possibilities, the second conditional is used to express unlikely or impossible situations, and
the third conditional refers to the past. Other combinations are
possible too and are known as mixed conditionals.

Match the numbers on the left with the letters on the right to
complete the sentences:

1.   Had I known all the facts before   a. I don't know what I'd
     the meeting,   do.
2.   If I didn't have a wife and   b. I'll have no choice but
     children to support,   to ask you to leave.
3.   If the talks come to nothing   c. I'd walk out of the job
     again,   today.
4.   If you're hoping to make a good   d. please do not hesitate
     impression on the new boss,   to contact us.
5.   If you're the sort of person   e. the advantage is that
     who's afraid of hard work,   you save both time and
6.   If you can work from home,   money.
7.   If you hadn't been so inflexible,   f. then I wouldn't have
8.   If you hadn't turned up late for   come unstuck the way
     the interview,   that I did.

9. If you miss this opportunity,
10. If you produced shoddy work like that for me,
11. If you want to find a good job,
12. If you were dissatisfied with the goods for any reason,
13. Should you have any further questions,
14. Unless you change your attitude,
15. Were I to be made redundant,

g. then some form of industrial action will be inevitable.

h. then you really can't expect to get very far.

i. we could have completed the deal.

j. you might have got the job.

k. you really need to learn the language first.

l. you'll really have to do a lot better than that.

m. you'll regret it for the rest of of your life.

n. you'd be entitled to a full refund.

o. you wouldn't last a day in the job.

E-mail Etiquette

Read through the following tips on email etiquette and then replace the missing linking words:

Additionally / although / as soon as /because / because / but also / However / if / in case / not only / or even / so as to / so that / Where / which

Remember that 1. ..... email is informal, you are always sending a note to one or more other people, and all the normal "rules" of behaviour apply. 2. ..... you only have the written word to convey every nuance of what you want to say, you need to think more carefully about it and consider where ambiguities may cause offence.

A message goes 3. ..... you press the Send button, 4. ..... means you cannot call it back if you have second thoughts. So best be sure you have all your second thoughts first. Read messages carefully before sending – 5. ...... they are offensive, or you have misspelled something. 6. ......, make sure you ask permission before forwarding or copying other people's messages 7. ..... there is no risk of upsetting them. You 8. ..... need to avoid sexist or racist language, 9. ..... to avoid using all upper case letters as this makes it look as if you are shouting.

10. ..... the message is very important, controversial or open to misunderstanding consider a face-to-face discussion instead. And do not assume that all outrageous messages are intended to inflame opinion 11. ..... they may instead be a clumsy attempt at humour, 12. ..... just the result of a lack of familiarity with the medium.

Describe the content of your message clearly in the "Subject" line

55

13. ..... help people to prioritise and to find information again later.

Send short messages that can be clearly understood on their own. 14. ....., do not send a short message as an attachment 15. ..... it wastes time opening two emails instead of one.

Adjectives with Dependent Prepositions (i)

Match the numbers on the left with the letters on the right to complete the sentences, like the example.

Example: **1-i**

1. **I'm not used**
2. Over the coming year we're quietly confident
3. She's clearly intent
4. He's not satisfied
5. If you're keen
6. You must be completely fed up
7. I know you're not in the habit
8. I'm not opposed
9. It's not that I'm averse
10. I'm really enthusiastic
11. I'm not generally noted

a. about having the opportunity to collaborate with you on the project and feel sure it will work out really well.

b. for losing my temper but you have a way of really annoying me I'm afraid.

c. of being able to turn the current deficit into a profit.

d. of working so late but I'm afraid you have no choice in the matter.

e. on making the move a permanent one, you'll need to show me you're up to the job.

f. on reaching the top and she's not going to let anyone stand in her way. That's what I admire about her.

g. to being given feedback, it's just the negative way in which you did it that upset me.

h. to giving you a pay rise. It's just that we can't afford to at this particular moment in time.

i. to having to get up so early in the morning and I'm finding it a bit of a strain.

j. with being a bit-part player as he feels he's got leadership potential.

k. with having to do so much overtime and looking forward to having a break from all this.

Adjectives with Dependent Prepositions (ii)

Match the numbers on the left with the letters on the right to complete the sentences, like the example.

Example: **7-i**

1. Although I was involved
2. Instead of being obsessed
3. My boss has such high expectations of me that I'm worried
4. The room's not suitable
5. Don't be too optimistic
6. I'm not going to be rushed
7. **If you're committed**
8. With so many people in the company having been laid off already, I'm resigned
9. Due to the dire financial straits we find ourselves in, we've been reduced
10. I'm not generally known
11. As you're so opposed

a. about getting the job because the other applicants seemed to be a lot better qualified than you.
b. about not being able to live up to them.
c. for dismissing staff but in your case I feel it's fully justified in view of what you've done.
d. for holding the meeting in because it's just not big enough.
e. in making the decision, it wasn't me who had the final say.
f. into making a decision so you're just going to have to be patient with me.
g. to having to go into liquidation.

h.   to losing my job eventually too.

i.   **to making a go of it then you really mustn't let yourself get discouraged so easily.**

j.   to taking part in the event, you'd better let the organisers know so they can give your place to someone else who does want to go.

k.   with making money all the time, what about trying to enjoy life for a change?

Homonyms (i)

A homonym is a word that has both the same sound and spelling as another but is different in meaning.

Find the pairs of homonyms that fit into these sentences:

1. I hope you'll be ..... and to the point because I'm an extremely busy woman.
    My ..... was to complete the work within the deadline and that is what I have done.

2. Between you and me although I've applied for the ....., I don't really hold out much hope and I just did so because I thought it would be useful practice.
    I'm sorry about the delay but I promise you the contract is now in the ..... and it should be with you by tomorrow at the latest.

3. I wouldn't mention the problem if I were you because it would be safer to let sleeping dogs .....
    If you ....., you'll be found out in then end so it really isn't worth it.

4. Discrimination in the workplace on the grounds of ..... is against the law.
    In order to meet the deadline, it's going to be a ..... against time.

5. I know the deal seems to be done and dusted but don't ..... your chickens before they're hatched because you could still be disappointed.
    If you're going to work for me, I need to know I can ..... on you.

6. You'll have to ..... me off your list I'm afraid because something else has cropped up since the last time we spoke and I won't be able to attend after all.
    Having such a major responsibility must be a heavy .....

to bear.

7. It's a great opportunity and you mustn't miss it. You need to ..... while the iron is hot.

Unless the two sides can come to an agreement, it looks like the workers could well vote to go on .....

8. I hope you don't ...., but I'm afraid I'll have to ask you to fill out another form.

You seem to have a lot on your ..... these days and your work is beginning suffer as a result. Perhaps you need to talk to someone about it.

9. Sooner or later you're going to have to ..... up to the situation whether you like it or not.

Instead of talking over the phone, what we really need is a .....-to-..... meeting.

10. Despite the fact that you treated me like dirt when I worked for you, I'm not the ..... of person to bear a grudge and I won't let what happened cloud my judgement now that the roles have been reversed.

The reason why I felt it was better to tell you the truth is that sometimes you have to be cruel to be ..... in situations like this.

The Perils of Mixing Business with Pleasure

Choose the best answer from each pair of alternatives. In most cases, only one of the answers is correct, but sometimes they both might be suitable. So be careful!

I know it's not something to be proud 1 <u>in / of</u> but I'm afraid I have to 2 <u>admit / confess</u> that 3 <u>they / there</u> have been 4 <u>occasions / times</u> when I have mixed business with pleasure, and had 5 <u>relations / relationships</u> with people I've worked with. Hopefully now I'm both older and wiser, I would not make such 6 <u>errors / mistakes </u>of judgement again. 7 <u>However / Moreover,</u> when we're young and 8 <u>led / ruled</u> by our hearts instead of our 9 <u>brains / heads,</u> we do tend to act rashly at times. We then find out 10 <u>at our own expense / to our cost</u> that all we have succeeded 11 <u>in doing / to do</u> is to put our jobs at risk, for one or even 12 <u>both / the both</u> of the persons involved can end up 13 <u>being dismissed / to be dismissed</u> in such situations. And even 14 <u>if / though</u> this is not 15 <u>a / the</u> case, it could still well 16 <u>lead to / result in</u> one of them feeling they have to hand in their 17 <u>notice / notices</u> as a result of what has 20 <u>expired / transpired</u>. This is why I urge you in the strongest possible 23 <u>conditions / terms</u> to make sure you don't fall 24 <u>into / through</u> this trap, for work and pleasure definitely don't mix!

Homonyms (ii)

Find the pairs of homonyms that fit into these sentences:

1. If I wasn't so ....., I'd lend you the money myself but I haven't got a penny.
   Once the talks ..... down, we were left with no other option.
2. If you stand for election, I'll ..... you all the way.
   I have to go away on business but I should be ..... by the end of the week.
3. Being true to ....., he turned up late for the meeting, just as I knew he would.
   She seems just the ..... of person we're looking for and I'm sure she'll be a great asset to the company.
4. The abbreviation Co. stands for .....
   Two's ..... but three's a crowd.
5. What a .....mess you've got me into! I should never have listened to your crazy idea.
   The penalty for breaking the health and safety regulations would be a hefty ......
6. I don't want to speak out of turn but, if you don't ..... my saying so, I think you're being a bit too hasty and perhaps you need to reconsider the idea.
   If this design is not what you're looking for, then I wonder what exactly you did have in .....
7. They say you can't judge a ..... by its cover but I'm not sure if that's true.
   I tried to ..... you a room in your usual hotel but I'm afraid it was completely full.
8. These negotiations have been dragging on for far too long and it's time we brought matters to a ......
   As you have more experience than anyone else of this kind of work, I'd like you to ..... the team.

9.   I'd like to ..... up the meeting for next Tuesday if that's all right with you.

I'm in a real ..... and I could do with some help.

10.   What's the current ..... of exchange between the dollar and and the pound?

At this ....., we're never going to get the job finished. We really need to get a move-on.

Fair Trade

Choose the most appropriate answer from each pair of alternatives. But be careful because sometimes both choices may be correct!

When you 1) do / make your weekly shopping, do you ever stop 2) considering / to consider 3) weather / whether the people 4) that / who produced the goods were paid a 5) fair / fair wage for the 6) work / works they 7) did / made? And are you willing to pay a bit extra to 8) assure / ensure that this is the case or is your only concern to pay as little as you possibly can regardless of how this might 9) affect / effect 10) the others / others less fortunate 11) as / than yourself? I suppose 12) a / the question that's really being asked here is 13) if / whether you can live with your 14) conscience / conscious or 15) no / not. That's why I've decided to 16) do / make a 17) conscious / conscientious effort to stop 18) buying / to buy goods in certain shops 19) that / which I know stock such products even 20) if / though they are invariably cheaper. And if 21) another / other people 22) do / make the same, perhaps we can bring 23) about / off a real change to consumer 24) customs / habits that will be of benefit 25) for / to all of us.

How much attention do you pay to whether the people who produce the food you buy were paid a fair amount of money for the job? Are there any products you refuse to buy for this reason? And how can we stop the exploitation of workers in developing countries from taking place?

Noun Phrases with Dependent Prepositions (ii)

Match the numbers on the left with the letters on the right to complete the following sentences:

1. I have no intention
2. If you're as fed up with your job as you say you are, I see absolutely no point
3. I have no hesitation at all
4. Unscrupulous people have no qualms
5. When I'm on the phone, I have difficulty
6. I'm in no mood
7. I've been her for over a year and I'm looking forward now
8. The problem with the job is the early start as I'm not in the habit
9. If you are in two minds
10. You have a real flair
11. To tell you the truth, I was on the point
12. I need to speak to the person who's in charge

a. about cheating others as I've found out to my cost.

b. about taking the job, don't make any decision just yet.

c for learning languages so I'm sure you'll pick it up really quickly.

d. for messing around so let's get straight down to business.

e. in recommending you as I'm sure you'll be a great asset to the company.

f. in understanding what people say and have to keep saying "pardon" all the time.

g. in your staying here.

h. of employing you if that's the way you behave.

i. of handing in my notice but at the last minute I decided to stay on.

j. of having to get up so early in the morning.

k. of ordering the stationery because we have no headed paper left.

l. to going back home and being able to see my family again.

What makes a good Leader?

Choose the best answer from each pair of alternatives. In most cases, only one of the answers is correct, but sometimes they both might be suitable. So be careful!

1 An / The answer to this question is 2 worth / worthy of its weight in 3 diamonds /gold. 4 In my opinion / If you ask me, a good leader is someone 5 who / that 6 conducts / leads 7 by / with example, but at 8 same / the same time has the 9 capability / ability to delegate. 10 Another / Other requirement for the 11 job / work is clearly good 12 communication / communicative skills. 13 Beside / Besides these 14 attributes / qualities, he or she 15 also would / would also benefit 16 from / of vision, originality and attention to 17 detail / details. 18 Being / To be able to 19 handle / handle with awkward members of 20 staff / stuff is a great asset too. When deadlines have to be met, I would also expect a good leader to roll up his or her 21 sleeves / trouser legs and get 22 down / up to work just like everyone else in the company is required to do in such situations. 23 Moreover / However, I would be interested to know what your opinion 24 of / on the subject is and what you 25 consider / regard to be important.

Adjectives with Dependent Prepositions (iii)

Match the numbers on the left with the letters on the right to complete the following sentences:

1. I know you're keen
2. If you hope to succeed in this company, you'll have to get used
3. The problem with you is that you're much too fond
4. I'm dissatisfied
5. You don't need to be concerned
6. You must be fed up
7. Although my critics have accused me
8. I got so absorbed
9. If you're opposed
10. Ambitious people are intent
11. In this company we're committed
12. As P.A. to the Managing Director, I'm responsible

a. about being made redundant because I can assure you there's absolutely no danger at all of that happening.

b. for seeing to all her travel arrangements.

c. in studying the report that I completely lost track of the time.

d. of being ruthless, I would say I'm just extremely determined.

e. of gossiping and it's going to get you into a lot of trouble one of these days.

f. on reaching the top and let nothing stand in their way.

g. on using your initiative, but it's not the way things work here.

h. to being a team player.

i. to saving energy, which is why all of us cycle to work.

j. to your savings being used to support the arms industry, then you should switch to an ethical bank.

k. with having to travel such long distances to work every day and it's a pity you can't find anything closer.

l. with merely playing a junior role in the company and feel it's time I was given a more responsible position.

One Word, Three Uses (iii)

Find one word only which can be used appropriately in all three sentences. Here is an example:

You've been overworking recently and you really need to ..... a break.

Perhaps the most sensible thing to do would be to ..... some time out to reconsider your position before you come to any decisions regarding your future.

There's been a great improvement in the company's figures and it is sales team who should ..... most of the credit for it.

Answer: take.

Q1

It's a guaranteed money-making scheme and if you invest in it, you should ..... a fortune.

What do you ..... of the new Director? She seems to know what she's doing but it's still early days yet.

I'm hopeful that the new proposals will ..... a real difference to our finances and put the company back on an even keel again.

Q2

I cannot possibly do all this work on my own so I was wondering whether you could ..... me a hand.

..... me the opportunity to work for you and I can assure you that you won't regret it.

These are our plans for the coming year and I hope you will ..... us your support.

Q3

You didn't ..... up much of a fight, did you? I thought you were more determined.

We need to ..... an end to this in-fighting once and for all because it's extremely damaging.

Now that you have proved how useful you are to the company, I think you have every right to ... in for a rise.

Q4

If you do not ..... up with the mortgage repayments, your house may be repossessed.

We need to ..... a tight rein on expenditure this year if we are to survive the current crisis.

You need to make sure you ..... out of trouble and that you don't rock the boat in any way.

Q5

If I am expected to ..... all the groundwork, then it only seems fair that I should get some of the credit for it.

I wonder if you could ..... me a favour and check these figures for me to make sure I have made no mistakes.

One of the problems with being a teacher these days is all the paperwork you now have to .....

Q6

As soon as you ..... me the go-ahead, I hope to put the plan into action.

To show you the confidence we have in your ability, we have decided to ... you a completely free rein and to let you do whatever you want.

I hope you approve of our plans that consequently you will ..... us your full backing.

Linking Words (ii)

Match the numbers on the left with the letters on the right to complete the sentences, like the example.

Example: **2-e**

1. Considering how hard you've worked,
2. **Whatever you say is not going to make any difference**
3. As long as you proceed with caution,
4. While I can't say I agree with you,
5. The changes being proposed are essential,
6. Despite the fact that the business is now doing better than it previously was,
7. As a result of the restructuring of the company,
8. In view of how many times you have been late this month,
9. In an attempt to find out what happened to the missing money,
10. Even though we've made considerable strides,
11. On account of the mounting cost of the raw materials required to produce the beverage,
12. Notwithstanding the fact that the proposal clearly has potential,
13. Regarding your request for a transfer,

a. a certain number of redundancies are unfortunately inevitable.
b. a further financial commitment at this point in time is unfortunately just not feasible.
c. a price rise now seems inevitable.
d. but I can assure you we will do our best to retain as many of you as possible.

e. **because the matter has already been settled.**

f. I can assure you we will leave no stone unturned.

g. I do understand your point of view.

h. in order for us to be able to compete with rival firms.

i. my response to your request for a pay rise must surely be obvious.

j. the best is surely still to come.

k. we're still not out of the woods yet.

l. we hope to get back to you with an answer by the end of next week at the latest.

m. you really deserve your current success.

n. you should have nothing to worry about.

Differentiating between Wants and Needs

Choose the best answer from each pair of alternatives. In most cases, only one of the answers is correct, but sometimes they both might be suitable. So be careful!

I cannot for 1) <u>a / the</u> life of me work out why but it seems as 2) <u>if / though</u> 3) <u>the more / most</u> I earn, 4) <u>the more / the most</u> I spend. At this 5) <u>rate / speed</u>, I'm always going to be in a financial mess. 6) <u>A / The</u> solution to the problem 7) <u>lays / lies</u> in being able to differentiate 8) <u>among / between</u> wants and needs. There are of course a great 9) <u>deal of / many</u> things we would all like to have and we see them 10) <u>advertised / advertising</u> on TV every day. 11) <u>However / Moreover,</u> 12) <u>apart from / as well as</u> water, food, shelter, and love, there are 13 <u>a few / few</u> things in 14 <u>life / the life</u> we actually need. So if we can wean ourselves 15) <u>from / off</u> all the unnecessary luxuries we 16) <u>appear / seem</u> to have become addicted to, it should then be possible to keep spending within a 17) <u>reasonable / sensible</u> limit and the problems that many of us are 18) <u>currently / presently</u> 19) <u>faced / wrestling</u> with, not only me, will then become a thing of the past.

If, on 20) <u>another / the other</u> hand, my 21) <u>argument / quarrel</u> has failed to convince you, and the compulsion to spend money still remains, then 22) at <u>last / least</u> consider 23) <u>giving / to give</u> it to charity instead of wasting it so that 24) <u>others / the others</u> more needy than you can have the 25) <u>opportunity / possibility</u> to benefit from your good fortune, and help to make the world a better place.

Linking Words (iii)

Match the numbers on the left with the letters on the right to complete the sentences, like the example.

Example: **2-1**

1. Notwithstanding the fact that the proposal clearly has potential,
2. **Regarding your request for a transfer,**
3. Due to a design fault,
4. Owing to events beyond our control,
5. Apart from there being a couple of minor initial problems,
6. While I obviously sympathize with you,
7. As well as there being complaints about the long hours,
8. In spite of suggestions to the contrary,
9. Unfortunately however hard I try,
10. Whatever might seem to be the case,
11. I'll phone everyone concerned to explain the change in the arrangements so as to
12. We have had to amend our original plans because of

a. a further financial commitment at this point in time is unfortunately just not feasible.
b. all the extra expenses we have incurred.
c. circumstances could well change again, which is why we still can't say we're out of the woods just yet.
d. I'm afraid there's little I can do to help.
e. I have no intention whatsoever of selling my stake in the company and all the rumours suggesting otherwise are simply untrue.
f. I just can't seem to get it right for some reason.

g. it has become necessary to recall the product. So if you have purchased one recently, please return it to the shop where you bought it and you will given a complete refund.

h. make sure there is no confusion.

i. the negotiations went really well in the end.

j. the rate of pay on offer was considered to be unacceptable too.

k. we have been forced to introduce some changes to the scheme.

l. **we hope to get back to you with an answer by the end of next week at the latest.**

How Assertive Are You?

1. How often do you upset people because of what you say or do?
a. often
b. sometimes
c. never

2. When was the last time you hit somebody?
a. within the last month
b. within the last year
c. more than a year ago

3. How often do you shout at your partner to get your own way?
a. often
b. sometimes
c. never

4. How do you react if others are hurt by things you say?
a. feel guilty for a long time afterwards
b. tell yourself to be more careful next time
c. forget about it

5. Have you ever made a colleague cry as a result of things you have said?
a. more than once
b. only once
c. never

6. Do you find it difficult to trust people?
a. never
b. sometimes
c. often

7. Have you ever been in trouble for acts of bullying or physical violence?

a. yes

b. no

8. How often do you lose your temper with waiters, bus drivers, or shop assistants?

a. often

b. sometimes

c. never

9. How do you behave when you feel passionately about an issue?

a. try to impose your ideas on others

b. lose your temper

c. accept that others may not feel the same way

10. Do you hate losing arguments?

a. yes

b. no

11. How often do you lose control completely when you get angry?

a. often

b. sometimes

c. never

12. Do other people ever seem scared to give you their opinions?

a. often

b. sometimes

c. never

Giving Presentations

Choose the most appropriate answer from each pair of alternatives. But be careful because sometimes both choices may be correct!

1) If / When you give a presentation, the 2) gold / golden rule is never to put yourself 3) down / out and never to apologize. The last thing you want is for your audience to 4) loose / lose confidence in you and you need to show you believe in yourself or you can't 5) except / expect others to. Secondly, you need to 6) assure / ensure you stick to the time limit and you don't overrun, not only to 7) avoid / prevent rubbing the organisers up the wrong way but also for the sake of the speaker due to follow you. The last thing you want is to be 8) considered / regarded as a bore so in addition to 9) know / knowing your subject, you also need to be able to put your knowledge across. This could well mean 10) to use / using audio-visual aids and even telling a few jokes 11) every now and then / from time to time. Although you'll undoubtedly want to give your audience something 12) fruity / meaty to get their 13) minds / teeth into, it's 14) best / the best not to overload them with material or the danger is it could go in one ear and out of 15) another / the other. As for 16) avoiding / preventing your 17) nerve / nerves from getting the better of you, the more opportunities you have to 18) practice / practise, the 19) easier easiest it will get. And all that 20) remains / rests is for me to wish you the very best of luck.

The Environmental Impact of Packaging

What do you do with packaging once you get home with your shopping and remove it? How about the situation in your country? Is the problem dealt with in a better or a worse way? What changes would you like to see take place? Read through the following passage about the environmental impact of packaging to find the missing prepositions:

More than half of packaging is plastic, which can take hundreds of years to break 1. _____ and can release harmful chemicals 2. _____ the environment during the process. The retailers who sell us this packaging have come 3. _____ increasing scrutiny. The more that people try and 4. _____ their recycling goals at home, particularly plastic, the more they seem to be left 5. _____, and this has deflected back 6. _____ the retailers.
Market research shows that customers want great quality products that look good, that taste good, the very highest quality. But they are also increasingly concerned 7._____ the impact of the packaging 8._____ the environment. However, retailers cannot get rid 9. _____ packaging entirely since it protects products, which thus get to the consumer 10._____ good condition. And surprisingly, if packaging was abandoned altogether, then the amount of food waste could increase, which 11. _____ turn could have an adverse environmental effect. Rotting food is a major source of methane, a gas which contributes 12. _____ global warming. After reducing the amount retailers use as much as possible, the next step is to try and ensure what they do use can be reused or recycled.
High Street retailers are experimenting 13. _____ green packaging. For example, one chain of retailers has introduced compostable salad bowls and high-tech composite materials 14. _____ its sandwich packets.
But is it enough? The efforts that retailers are making to reduce

packaging are a start, but it is going to take some time 15. _____ the problem is solved and it is clearly not something that can be done overnight.

***

Study these two sentences:

a. *The retailers who sell us packaging have come under increasing scrutiny.*
b. *The retailers, who sell us packaging, have come under increasing scrutiny.*

The sentence that contains the non-defining clause, with extra information, indicates that all retailers have come under increasing scrutiny. The sentence that contains the defining clause, with essential information, indicates that only the retailers who sell us packaging have been affected. Which is which?

Now complete the rules:

Defining clauses contain 1. ..... information without which the sentence is incomplete. Non-defining clauses contain 2. ..... information that is not essential. 3. ..... clauses have no commas whereas 5. ..... do have commas and are found mainly in 6. ..... English.

When talking about persons we use the relative pronoun 7. ..... and when talking about things we use the linking word WHICH. The word THAT can be used for both people and things but is never found in 8. ..... clauses as can be seen from the following example:

More than half of packaging is plastic, which can take hundreds of years to break down and can release harmful chemicals into the environment during the process.

Phrasal Nouns (i)

What do you do to **turn off** at the end of the day?
You might have found the presentation of interest but for me it was a complete **turn-off**.

Phrasal nouns can be made from certain phrasal verbs as in the example above. Sometimes the phrasal noun is hyphenated and sometimes the two parts form a new word. Sometimes the root of the verb is placed first (turn-off) but sometimes it comes at the end (outset). Incidentally, there are also phrasal adjectives, such as takeover (a takeover bid)

Now complete the following sentences with suitable phrasal nouns:

1. People have had enough and if the Chancellor attempts to increase Income Tax yet again, there is likely to be a public ..... (CRY)
2. Though the annual ..... of the company has increased, profits have actually fallen due to a rise in the cost of raw materials. (TURN)
3. Once the new machinery has been installed in the factory, we are hopeful that it should lead to a significant increase in ...... (PUT)
4. In the ..... to the next Election, the Chancellor would be well advised to introduce some tax cuts. (RUN)
5. The differences between the two sides seem to be irreconcilable and it looks as if they're heading for a ..... (SHOW)
6. It's only fair that there should be an equal ..... of the profits between us as we each did 50% of the work. (SHARE)
7. There's been a ..... in profits over the last quarter but we're hopeful that business will soon pick up again.

(TURN)

8. Despite the current economic recession, the ..... for the future looks extremely promising. (LOOK)

9. I wonder what the ..... of the talks will be. Let's hope both sides can finally reach an agreement this time. (COME)

10. Unfortunately there has been a ..... at this end due to a national rail strike but we are hoping to be able to send you the goods by the end of the week and they should be with by next Monday. (HOLD)

Cold-Calling

Choose the best answer from each pair of alternatives. In most cases, only one of the answers is correct, but sometimes they both might be suitable. So be careful!

1 <u>A</u> / The fact of the matter is that if I want to buy something, I will go out and look 2 <u>at</u> / <u>for</u> it so cold-calling 3 <u>on</u> / <u>to</u> me is a total 4 loss / <u>waste</u> of time. 5 <u>Moreover</u> / <u>Nevertheless,</u> the people who are unfortunate enough to have to do this for a 6 life / <u>living</u> 7 <u>appear</u> / <u>seem</u> to be oblivious to this. I 8 <u>wander</u> / <u>wonder</u> how you 9 <u>deal</u> / <u>tackle</u> with 10 <u>a</u> / <u>the</u> problem. When door-to-door salesmen 11 <u>assure</u> / <u>ensure</u> you that they won't take up much of your time, you know that is 12 <u>exactly</u> / <u>precisely</u> what they will do. And if they 13 <u>say</u> / <u>tell</u> that "I'm sure you'll find what I have to say interesting", then you can be equally sure that it will not be. 14 <u>However</u> / <u>Moreover,</u> for some reason they just never seem to get 15 <u>a</u> / <u>the</u> message. What they fail to understand about people like me is that the 16 <u>more</u> / <u>most</u> they persist, the 17 <u>more</u> / <u>most</u> certain it is that I won't buy anything at all from them. 18 <u>As</u> / <u>Like</u> many the majority of people I know, I do not respond to this kind of approach so why on earth do people do such 19 <u>jobs</u> / <u>works</u>? The answer of 20 <u>coarse</u> / <u>course</u> is that many of them work for nothing more than a basic 21 <u>salary</u> / <u>wage</u> and have to depend on the commission they earn to make enough to live on, and this helps to explain why they are so desperate. I suppose we should feel sorry 22 <u>about</u> / <u>for</u> them. 23 <u>However</u> / <u>Moreover,</u> when you get woken up on Sunday morning at seven o' clock by someone trying 24 <u>selling</u> / <u>to sell</u> you already have, or have absolutely no use 25 <u>at all</u> / <u>whatsoever</u> for, you tend to forget this!

Phrasal Nouns (ii)

Now complete the following sentences with suitable phrasal nouns:

1. I've heard he is talking about making a ....., but his reputation has been so tarnished that the prospect of that happening must surely be extremely remote. (COME)
2. The firm pleaded guilty earlier this month to breaching food and hygiene regulations in relation to an ..... of food poisoning. (BREAK)
3. I don't want anything to go wrong when we meet the delegation at the airport so we had better have a second car on ...... in case anything should go wrong. (STAND)
4. Having our headquarters in a listed building certainly impresses visitors but the cost of ...... of the property is considerable, and the reason why we are now considering the possibility of relocating. (KEEP)
5. We weren't expecting many of the shareholders to attend the meeting but the ..... was quite impressive in the end. (TURN)
6. Instead of sitting glued to the computer screen all day, what you really need is a ..... in the gym. (WORK)
7. The admission by the CEO that he might indeed have made a mistake was regarded as a ...... as he was normally not the sort of person ever to admit that he might have been wrong. (CLIMB)
8. There's too much junk in this office and not enough space to work in. What is needed is a good ..... (CLEAR)
9. I need to make a quick ..... this evening because I'm going to the theatre straight after work. (GET)
10. After the first week of the course there were one or two ....., but most of the participants completed the full programme. (DROP)

A Model Presentation

Match the numbers with the letters to complete the sentences, and then place them in the correct order:

1. As we still have a few minutes left,

2. Before I start, for anyone not familiar with the subject,

3. But if you'd still like to talk some more,

4. Even though not everyone's arrived yet,

5. Finally I'd like to

6. First of all, I'd like to

7. For any of you have found this presentation a bit confusing,

8. I can see outside the door that the next speaker is waiting to set up

9. Now that we've dealt with the theory,

10. Perhaps I should also point out before I get going

a. I think we'd better start as there's a great deal to cover and time is limited.

b. I'd like to provide you with some background information.

c. let's consider how it can be applied in practice.

d. not to worry because I'm now going to run through the main points again.

e. say how much I've enjoyed working with you today and I hope we'll have the chance to do so again some time.

f. so I think we'd better stop the questions there to give her the time to do so.

g. thank you all for coming along and I hope you'll find the session useful.

h. you don't need to take notes as it's all on the hand-outs you'll be given at the end of the session.

i. you might like to take the opportunity to ask any questions you have.

j. you're more than welcome to join me outside in the bar where we can do so over a drink or two.

Ethical Sourcing

A cause for concern is whether the goods being sold in our shops are ethically sourced or not. Read through the following passage that deals with the subject to find the missing prepositions.

Sustainable sourcing 1. ..... the goods they sell is one of the most important issues facing the supermarkets. Customers are demanding that more 2. ..... what they buy is sourced 3. ..... an environmentally sustainable way.

In the Shetland Islands, supermarkets are tackling the problem of sustainable sourcing of cod, Britain's favourite fish.

Our love of cod has contributed 4. ..... an ecological disaster. Since the Second World War, more and more fish were trawled 5. ..... the North Sea and the other seas around Britain: more than the cod stocks could bear. As a result, around Britain we have hunted cod 6. ..... the brink of extinction. The stocks are 7. ..... historic low levels and the fisheries barely economically viable.

Supermarkets used to sell masses of cheap cod 8. ..... little regard 9. ..... its sustainability. But now the cod has nearly gone, some supermarkets; Sainsbury's, Marks & Spencer, Waitrose and Tesco; are taking action. They now won't take any cod caught from the North Sea, and will only buy cod that that has been caught from sustainable stocks.

In the Shetland Islands, Johnson Seafarms has set up the world's first commercial cod farming operation. The fish are farmed organically in pens in the open sea. It supplies Sainsbury's and Tesco.

Emphasising its sustainable credentials, the cod is marketed as "No Catch Cod".

But farmed organic cod is expensive to produce. It takes three years to rear a fish. Farmed cod retails 10. ..... almost twice the price of other fresh cod. Also it is doubtful if farming can 11. ..... its own meet current demands 12. ..... cod.

And it is not just cod that is 13. ..... threat. According 14. ..... the WWF, the problem over fish stocks is a global one. They estimate that 75% of fish stocks are actually over-exploited and that the stocks of the oceans' top fish - fish such as tuna, marlin, cod, flounder, halibut – has been depleted by 15. ..... to 90%.

What is clear is that if the fish we eat is going to be sustainable 16. ..... the future, then it is going to become a much rarer and more expensive food. The question is: are customers going to be willing to pay the true cost?

One Word, Three Uses (iv)

Find one word only which can be used appropriately in all three sentences. Here is an example:

You've been overworking recently and you really need to ..... a break.

Perhaps the most sensible thing to do would be to ..... some time out to reconsider your position before you come to any decisions regarding your future.

There's been a great improvement in the company's figures and it is sales team who should ..... most of the credit for it.

Answer: take.

Q1

If I were you, I'd ..... sleeping dogs lie and I wouldn't risk raising the subject again.

As you know, I'm depending on you so please don't ..... me down

Instead of selling the property, why don't you ..... it? The rent money you get each month will pay for your mortgage.

Q2

Unfortunately we find ourselves in a no-..... situation that nobody can benefit from.

I did my best to ..... them over to my way of thinking at the meeting but I'm afraid it was all in vain.

Don't worry about the legal costs because I'm prepared to represent you on a no ..... no fee basis.

Despite your being up against it, I have absolutely no doubt you'll ..... out in the end.

Q3

As for your salary, we'd like to be able to .... you more but I'm afraid we just can't afford to.

Although we made an ..... on the property, it wasn't accepted because someone else was prepared to pay the full asking price.
I'm looking for a job in sales but unfortunately there's nothing on ..... at the moment

Q4

Work has fallen behind schedule and we'll need to ..... up all this lost time somehow.
Don't ..... out you don't know what I'm talking about. The fact of the matter is you know only too well.
I'd like to know what ..... of car the company will provide me with.
If you don't mind my asking, how much money do you actually ..... a week?

Q5

I'm sorry I forgot to call you but I have had a lot on my ..... just recently.
Now that you have assumed control, I wonder what changes you have in ..... for the company.
I have never heard such nonsense before. Whoever told you that was clearly not in their right .....
I have to go away on business for a few days so I wonder if you would ..... standing in for me.

Q6

An opportunity like this won't come round again in a hurry so we need to ..... while the iron is hot.
I know we did not ..... it off the first time we met but hopefully things will change once we get to know each other better.
It will save time if all the unsuitable candidates can be ..... off the list before we start the interview process.
When the talks between the management and the union broke down, the workers voted to go on .....

Q7

There has been an unfortunate misunderstanding and we need to ..... the air.

Now that you have taken the trouble to explain things to me everything is .....

If you ..... all your papers away, we'll have some space to work in here.

The doctors say you are now in the ..... so you have nothing more to worry about.

I don't know why anyone should confuse the two because there is a ..... difference between them.

Food Miles

Choose the most appropriate answer from each pair of alternatives. But be careful because sometimes both choices may be correct!

When did you last 1. look / watch to see where your food has come from? Our supermarkets stock apples from New Zealand, asparagus from Peru and beans from Kenya, and hundreds of other 2. lines / makes that have been brought from all over the world. It is estimated that 3. food / the food in an average shopping trolley has travelled 100,000 miles. Only a small but significant 4. proportion / share is imported by air, the 5. remains / rest coming by boat and lorry. Many products can be 6. grown / grown up in 7. U.K. / the UK, but only in 8. season / the season. Now we have 9. become / been used 10. to have / to having these products all year round, and this increases our 11. reliance / reliability on bringing in goods from abroad. But as 12. awareness / consciousness of the environmental impact of flying in goods grows, so it has become a priority for the supermarkets to try 13. reducing / to reduce it. 14. However / Moreover, is it that simple? If supermarkets stop 15. importing / to import from 16. developed / developing countries then it could have a detrimental impact in those countries by putting local workers, 17. that / who have whole families 18. dependant / dependent on them, out of work. This is why the solution to the problem is less clear cut 19. as / than it 20. firstly / at first it 21. may / might 22. appear / seem to be. We also need to 23. bare / bear in mind that 24. British the British grown 25. produce is / products are not necessarily more energy efficient. There are approximately 900 horticultural producers in this country using glasshouses that are artificially heated. And producers use enough extra energy in their greenhouses to supply 55,000 homes for a year.

Gerund or Infinitive?

Study the examples presented below, and then see if you can complete the rules:

You should stop spending so much money on branded goods.
You should stop to consider whether they are really worth the extra they cost.

Do you like being your own boss?
Wouldn't you like to work for a company instead of being self-employed?

When I was a student, nobody used to have a computer as they hadn't even been invented yet.
Now I'm so used to depending on a computer that I don't think I could manage without one any more.

I regret never having had the opportunity to work overseas but it was more difficult for me than for you as I don't speak any foreign languages.
I regret to inform you that your application has been unsuccessful.

You really should try to make more of an effort as you're in serious danger of losing this job.
Perhaps you should try working in some other field instead.

Being self-employed means having no job security.
I don't intend to be a sales assistant forever. I mean to find something better.

We advise investing your money for a period of no less than three years.

We advise you not to withdraw your money before then or you'll lose a great deal of interest.

STOP+ING is used to refer to an action 1. ..... in time but STOP TO DO is used to refer to the 2. ..... of a new action. Verbs that express 3. ..... and dislikes are followed by the gerund to refer to things in 4. ..... but the to-infinitive to refer to a 5. .....occasion. USED TO DO refers to a 5. ..... habit whereas BE / GET USED TO+ING to show you are 6. ..... with an action. Use TRY with the gerund to show something is an 7. ..... but TRY TO DO to talk about something that is 8. ..... to do. When MEAN is followed by the gerund, it is a synonym for 9. ..... but when it is followed by the to-infinitive it is used to refer to 10. ..... for the future. As for the verb ADVISE, it is only used with the to-infinitive when it is followed by an 11. ..... Another verb which works the same way as TO ADVISE is 12. .....

Now practise using the verbs by matching the numbers on the left with the letters on the right to complete the sentences:

1. You've been hard at work at it since this morning and it's time you stopped
2. You haven't stopped
3. You really must try
4. Why don't you try
5. I don't like
6. I wouldn't like
7. I'm not used to
8. I used to
9. We don't allow
10. We don't allow employees
11. Given the choice, I'd prefer
12. I don't like the idea of being self-employed. I prefer
13. He went on
14. After he'd shown me round the department, he went on

a. run my own company but unfortunately it went bust.
b. smoking or eating in the office.
c. being an employee
d. not to have to work at all.
e. to use the office phone for private calls either.
f. complaining ever since you started working here.
g. to be more economical.
h. to introduce me to the other members of staff.
i. being told what to do all the time, especially by you.
j. talking for ages and I couldn't get a word in edgeways.
k. to have a break.
l. to work for a boss like yours either.
m. lowering the price to increase demand for the product?
n. being given all the dirty to do.

One Word, Three Uses (v)

Find one word only which can be used appropriately in all three sentences. Here is an example:

You've been overworking recently and you really need to ..... a break.

Perhaps the most sensible thing to do would be to ..... some time out to reconsider your position before you come to any decisions regarding your future.

There's been a great improvement in the company's figures and it is sales team who should ..... most of the credit for it.

   Answer: take.

Q1

We can't go on squabbling like this all the time and we really need to ..... to some kind of an agreement.

I never expected anything like this to happen and it has ..... as a complete surprise to me.

My only hope is that perhaps something good will ..... out of all this mess in the end.

Q2

As you seem to ..... in the know, perhaps you can explain to me what exactly is going on.

I'm afraid our disagreement over this issue is always likely to ..... a bone of contention between us.

You seem to ..... in two minds about what to do which, in view of the situation, is hardly surprising.

Q3

This deal is really important to the company so it's essential you don't ..... a mess of it.

Together we need to ..... a stand against the corruption that seems to be endemic in this country.

I don't see how you can expect to ... any headway unless you're prepared for some changes.

Q4

Why do I always have to ..... all the dirty work? It really isn't fair.

As long as you ..... your best, nobody can possibly ask for any more than that.

Criticising your colleagues the way you've been doing won't ..... you any credit at all.

Q5

Is there a cashpoint machine near here? I need to ..... out some money.

We really like the new product. The only .....back is the price. And if it were cheaper, we wouldn't hesitate to place an order.

I hope she's not going to ..... out the opening speech as the audience is getting rather restless.

I wish we could ..... him into committing himself to the project but unfortunately he still seems rather hesitant.

Q6

Could you ..... me through to the Accounts Department please?

If we are to have any chance of success, we need to increase our out..... and, at the same time, to reduce costs somehow.

I find it difficult to ..... across my ideas in English because, as you probably know, it is not my native language.

Pet Hates

Choose the most appropriate answer from each pair of alternatives. But be careful because sometimes both choices may be correct!

There's nothing that annoys me more than unsolicited junk mail. Every morning I wake up to find my letterbox full 1) <u>of / with</u> it and it drives me 2) <u>crazy / stupid</u>, especially the letters that try 3) <u>persuading / to persuade</u> you to take out a loan. 4) <u>A / The</u> fact of the matter is that the vast majority of 5) <u>people / the people</u> can't possibly afford to ever pay such loans off and many even end up 6) <u>having / to have</u> their homes repossessed when they can't meet the repayments. We need to do more to protect the vulnerable and it's high time 7) <u>to introduce a law / a law was introduced</u> to stop this unethical form of advertising. And while I'm on 8) <u>a / the</u> subject, unsolicited newsletters from political parties get on my nerves too. Personally, I always make a point 9) <u>of returning / to return</u> them with a letter of complaint in an unstamped envelope so that the sender has to pay the postal charge at the other end and I advise you 10) <u>doing / to do</u> the same. That way, once and for all, we may be able to put a stop 11) <u>on / to</u> the 12) <u>practice / practise</u>. Not only is it unsolicited junk mail that makes me irate but also 13) <u>a / the</u> postal service. For it would 14) <u>appear / seem</u> that the more they increase the postal charges, the 15) <u>worse / worst</u> the delivery service seems to get. I remember 16) <u>getting / to get</u> three deliveries daily when I was a child but nowadays we're lucky if we even get one. 17) <u>However / Moreover</u>, to make matters even worse, the one delivery we do get usually contains other people's mail delivered to the wrong address, 18) <u>that / which</u> leaves me to 19) <u>wander / wonder</u> whether the postman is even 20) <u>legible / literate</u>. So what 21) <u>do I say / I say</u> is bring back the 22) <u>good old / old good</u> days. And while we're at it, why don't we ban 23) <u>private the private</u> cars too and make everyone 24) <u>to use / use</u> 25) <u>public / the public</u> transport instead? That way we can not only reduce traffic congestion but protect the environment too. But that's another subject.

TO + ING

Match the numbers on the left with the letters on the right to complete the sentences, like the example.

Example: **2-h**

1. We're looking for someone who is prepared to commit themselves
2. **I'm one hundred per cent dedicated**
3. I hope you find the proposal of interest and I look forward
4. If you're averse
5. I'm so short of money that I've been reduced
6. As I've been unable to find anything permanent, I've had to resign myself
7. In addition
8. Not being able to speak the language, I'm limited
9. Middle-aged businessmen who are overweight, smoke, and drink too much are prone
10. We're going to try placing an advert in the local newspaper with a view
11. If you confess
12. I can understand the way you must be feeling. I'd react badly
13. In view of how badly you've been let down before I can well understand why you're not disposed

a. to being criticised, then you're really not going to last very long in this job.
b. to being overqualified, unfortunately the applicant also came across as being rather arrogant.
c. to being treated that way too.
d. to doing nothing more than manual work for the time

being.

e. to drumming up more business.

f. to having heart attacks.

g. to having misappropriated company funds and resign forthwith, we are then prepared to drop all legal proceedings against you.

h. **to making a success of this company however much hard work it takes.**

i. to pawning all my family heirlooms in an effort to keep the wolves from the door.

j. to receiving your response.

k. to taking on a succession of temporary jobs since I arrived in this country.

l. to trusting anyone again.

m. to working long term for the company.

Phrasal Adjectives

I'm going to **pay** you **back** for all the trouble you've caused me even if it's the last thing I ever do.
I'll never forget how badly you treated me when I worked for you and now it is **payback** time. (PAY)

Phrasal nouns can be made from certain phrasal verbs. Sometimes the phrasal noun is hyphenated and sometimes the two parts form a new word. Sometimes the root of the verb is placed first (turn-off) but sometimes it comes at the end (outset). There are also phrasal adjectives, as you can see from the example above.

Now complete the following sentences with suitable phrasal adjectives:

1. I'm only prepared to sign the contract as long as there's a ….. clause. (GET)
2. Before you enter into any negotiations, it's important to establish a ….. position first in case things don't quite work out as planned. (FALL)
3. There have been a number of ….. bids for the company over the years but fortunately they have all been unsuccessful so far. (TAKE)
4. We can't keep pouring money into the scheme without any return so we need to establish a ….. point. (CUT)
5. I didn't expect you to behave like that. I thought you'd be more ….. about things. (GROW)
6. The new model of the car has been a ….. success and exceeded all the company's expectations. (RUN)
7. When you announced you were standing down, it came as a real ….. blow and it took us completely by surprise. (KNOCK)

8. I don't feel like cooking tonight and neither do you so let's order a ..... meal. (TAKE)
9. Why is it being sold at a ..... price? There must be something wrong with it. (GIVE)
10. If you win your case for wrongful dismissal as I expect you to do, you can look forward to a substantial ..... (PAY)

Answer Key

Visualizing your Ideal Job 1 bitching 2 and so on 3 as 4 wasting 5 on 6 visualizing 7 ideal 8 far / much 9 closer 10 about 11 they do 12 figured / worked 13 lies 14 paying / to pay 15 to 16 other 17 tune 18 on 19 yet 20 into 21 make 22 walk 23 chances / odds 24 minimal 25 prevent yourself 26 time 27 sights 28 aware / mindful 29 Count 30 ride

Verbs with Dependent Prepositions: 1-l / 2-g / 3-d / 4-m / 5-f / 6-e / 7-h / 8-j / 9-k / 10-c / 11-b / 12-i / 13-a

Crossword Puzzle (i): 1. Jack / 2. temporary / 3. unable / 4. hands / 5. redundant / 6. notice / 7. interview / 8. vitae / 9. fingers / 10. regret

Crossword Puzzle (ii): 1. gamble / 2. root / 3. invest / 4. debt / 5. play / 6. minimum / 7. earn / 8. mortgage / 9. trees / 10. fees / 11. overdraft / 12. cashpoint

Looking for a Job? – Get a Head Start 1curriculum vitae 2 the 3 hunting 4 employer 5 make a snap judgment 6 moment / second 7 to 8 edge 9 The 10 avoid 11 more than likely / probably 12 bin 13 making (an experiment which might not work) 14 to smudge (because it's difficult to do) 15 of getting 16 Start off 17 at 18 that / which 19 an outline 20 experience

The Odd One Out (i): 1. minimum wage / 2. tax rebate / 3. incapacity benefit / 4. annual increment / 5. redundancy pay / 6. Christmas bonus / 7. jobseekers allowance / 8. income support / 9. fringe benefits / 10. tax code

The odd word is **council**

Job-Hunting: 1. If / When 2. a job / work 3. most 4. if 5. trying 6. in 7. in feeling 8. for 9. absolutely 10. receiving 11. despite 12. However 13. setbacks 14. way 15. assure 16. in no doubt 17. by 18. problems / troubles 19. worrying 20. if 21. the end 22. to get 23. perspective 24. at 25. as long as / so long as

Writing a Covering Letter for a Job Application: 1a / 2b / 3a / 4a or b or c / 5b / 6c / 7 a or b or c or f / 8b or d / 9d / 10b

Uncountable Nouns: 1. music 2. health 3. publicity 4. Money 5. unemployment 6. stationery 7. progress 8. furniture 9. evidence 10. equipment 11. information 12. machinery 13. damage 14. food 15. advice 16. research 17. paperwork 18. spam

Plural Nouns: 1. savings 2. belongings 3. outskirts 4. goods 5. odds 6. minutes 7. straits 8. surroundings 9. takings 10. Contents 11. trousers 12. winnings 13. poor 14. congratulations 15. means 16. trousers 17. offspring

Ordering Activity: 1.c / 2.a / 3.b / 4.e / 5.d

Money Makes the World Go Round (i): 1-b 2-d 3-l 4-g 5-f 6-a 7-i 8-j 9.h 10-m 11-c 12-n 13-k 14-e

Money Makes the World Go Round (ii): 1-d 2-i 3-f 4-h 5-k 6-a 7-l 8-e 9-c 10-g 11-d 12-j

Uncountable Nouns: How to refer to them (i):
A CAUSE OF anxiety / distress / global warming / hardship / inflation / misery / poverty / trouble / misunderstanding / homelessness

A SUPPLY OF cash / electricity / energy / equipment / food / gas / information / medicine / money / stationery

1. stationery / 2. anxiety / 3. energy / 4. information / 5. conflict / 6. medicine / 7. inflation / 8. water

The Value of Savings: 1) not 2) trying 3) to build 4) who knows 5) lies 6) corner 7) point / use 8) by 9) such a 10) ripe 11) spending 12) it 13) will 14) However, 15) the 16) wrap 17) factor 18) account / consideration 19) in 20) rates

Uncountable Nouns: How to refer to them (ii):

A MEANS OF birth control / communication / discipline / government / identification / recruitment / self-assessment / supervision / support / taxation / waste disposal

A SOURCE OF amusement / comfort / energy / enlightenment / excellence / information / inspiration / joy / knowledge / pleasure / revelation / satisfaction

1. identification / 2. support / 3. energy / 4. information / 5. birth control / 6. government / 7. waste disposal / 8. revelation / 9. inspiration / 10. excellence

Stress at Work: 1. say 2. play 3. doubt 4. there 5. truth 6. do 7. there 8. price 9. such 10. After all 11. ensure 12. exercise 13. with 14. somewhat 15. dividends 16. body 17. mind 18. fewer 19. Furthermore 20. concern

One Word, Three Uses (i): Q1. stake Q2. cost Q3. deal Q4. bargain Q5. value Q6. price Q7. charge

How stressed out are you?
CHECK YOUR SCORES:

1 a-2 b-3 c-1	**2** a-1 b-2 c-3	**3** a-2 b-1 c-3
4 a-3 b-2 c-1	**5** a-1 b-3 c-2	**6** a-3 b-1 c-2

WHAT YOUR SCORE MEANS:

11 – 18 You clearly feel stressed out and need to do something about it. Make sure you do some regular exercise or take up meditation or yoga. Reduce your intake of stimulants such as nicotine and caffeine. Eat non-fatty, wholesome starchy foods and avoid sugars. And, most important of all, learn how to say no.

10 – 14 Your stress levels are about average, but you should do what you can to lower them so read the tips above.

6 – 9 You're doing well and have nothing to worry about. We live in a stressful world but it's obvious you can cope. You can set a good example for those around you to follow so they can learn how to keep their stress levels under control too.

Business or Economy Class? 1 seems / would seem 2 business travellers 3 are often 4 fares 5 far / much 6 practice 7 making 8 hardly any different to / almost identical to 9 that 10 economy 11 paying 12 three times 13 the 14 legroom 15 in 16 you / your 17 getting 18 any quicker / any more quickly 19 not 20 having 21 buy 22 them 23 footing / paying 24 However 25 advice

Writing a Formal Letter of Complaint: 1f / 2a or b or c or g / 3 a or c or d / 4 a or b or c or d / 5d / 6 a or b or c or d / 7c or e / 8c

Are you a good Traveller?
CHECK YOUR SCORE

1. a-5 b-10 c-0	2. a-0 b-5 c-10	3. a-10 b-0 c.5
4. a-5 b-0 c-10	5. a-5 b-0 c-10	6. a-0 b-10 c-5
7. a.0 b-10 c-5	8. a-10 b-5 c-0	9. a-10 b-5 c-0
10. a-10 b-5 c-0	11. a-0 b-10 c-5	12. a-0 b-5 c-10
13. a-0 b-5 c.10	14. a-0 b-10 c-5	15. a-0 b-5 c-10
16. a-5 b.10 c-0	17. a-10 b-5 c-0	18. a-10 b-0 c-5
19. a-0 b-5 c-10	20 a-10 b-5 c-0	

WHAT YOUR SCORE MEANS

140-200   You are an efficient traveller and you plan your schedule meticulously months in advance. But if anything does go wrong, it floors you. In fact, you spend so much time making sure that nothing will go wrong that you hardly have anytime left to enjoy yourself. Relax a little. You have to trust to luck sometimes, and it will give you more chance to have a good time.

70-135   Although you plan your travel and take care to avoid the obvious pitfalls, you are not the sort of person to spend sleepless nights worrying about it. And it is a formula that works for you most of the time. You probably have the occasional disappointment and upset, but we all do and you accept that this is how life goes. Whatever happens, you make the best of things because you know that the unexpected can turn out to be the most fun.

0-65   Every time you travel further than the end of your road, you put your life at risk because you do things on the spur of the moment and leave everything to chance. So you should not be surprised when you then end up in a mess. You try to storm your way through difficult moments but you can never win this way. Learn to plan the basics, and then you can relax and enjoy yourself more.

Using Low Emission forms of Transport: 1 The 2 affects 3 climate change 4 flying 5 altogether ("all together" means everyone to do something at the same time) 6 about 7 into 8 we asked 9 to fly 10 by / via 11 the future 12 to be 13 public transport (zero article to refer to a subject in general) 14 avoid 15 reduce 16 impact 17 driving 18 if / whether 19 journey 20 another 21 holiday ("vacation" is American English) 22 closer 23 abroad / overseas 24 taking 25 instead of / rather than

A Code of Ethics for Tourists: 1. in 2. with 3. about 4. of 5. on 6. to 7. of 8. in 9. from 10. of 11.for 12. through 13. with 14. of 15. of 16. on 17. from 18. on 19. of 20. to 21. out 22. on 23. in

Noun Phrases with Dependent Prepositions (i): 1-g/2-i/3-e/4-h/5-k/6-j/7-c/8-b/9-a/10-f/11-d/12-l

One Word, Three Uses (ii): Q1. business Q2. stock Q3. control Q4. company Q5. interest Q6. lease

Linking Words (i): 1-b / 2-c / 3-g / 4-j / 5-i/ 6-l / 7-h / 8-d / 9-a / 10-f / 11-j / 12-e/13-m

The odd one out (ii): 1. bank charges / 2. travellers cheques / 3. personal loan / 4. ethical investor / 5. cashpoint machine / 6. direct debit / 7. credit rating / 8. home insurance / 9. savings account / 10. overdraft limit

The odd word is **mortgage**

Discrimination in the Workplace: 1 broadest 2 discrimination 3 than 4 manifest 5 Direct 6 because of / on account of 7 consider / take 8 that / who 9 under 10 down 11 indirect 12 more subtle / subtler 13 there 14 which 15 leads to / results in 16 on the grounds of / for reasons of 17 in 18 asking 19 As 20 another 21 implementing 22 terms 23 intimidated 24 rid 25 practice

Homophones: 1a. weigh 1b. way / 2a. steel 2b. steal / 3a. right 3b. write / 4a. feat 4b. feet / 5a. hole 5b. whole / 6a. tied 6b. tide / 7a. cue 7b. queue / 8a. where 8b. wear / 9a. heir 9b. air / 10a. scene 10b. seen

Race, Sex and Marital Discrimination: 1. against 2. on 3. for 4. against 5. for 6. between 7. with 8. to 9. with 10. of 11. of 12. Under 13. against 14. on 15. at

Conditionals: 1-f 2-c 3-g 4-l 5-h 6-e 7-i 8-j 9-m 10-o 11-k 12-n 13-d 14-b 15-a

E-mail Etiquette: 1. although 2. Where 3. as soon as 4. which 5. in case 6. Additionally 7. so that 8. not only 9. but also 10. If 11. because 12. or even 13. so as to 14. However 15. because

Adjectives with Dependent Prepositions (i): 1-i / 2-c / 3-f / 4-j / 5-e / 6-k / 7-d / 8-h / 9-g / 10-a / 11-b

Adjectives with Dependent Prepositions (ii): 1-e / 2-k / 3-b / 4-d / 5-a / 6-f / 7-i / 8-h / 9-g / 10-c / 11-j

Homonyms (i): 1. brief / 2. post / 3. lie / 4. race / 5. count / 6. cross / 7. strike / 8. mind / 9. face / 10. Kind

The Perils of Mixing Business with Pleasure: 1 of 2 admit (to confess is usually something you do in court) 3 there 4 occasions

/ times 5 relationships 6 errors 7However 8 ruled 9 heads 10 to our cost 11 in doing 12 both 13 being 14 if 15 the 16 lead to / result in 17 notice 18 transpired 19 terms 20 into

Homonyms (ii): 1. broke / 2. back / 3. type / 4. company / 5. fine / 6. mind / 7. book 8. head / 9. fix / 10. rate

Fair Trade: 1. do 2. to consider 3. whether 4. that / who 5. fair 6. work 7. did 8. ensure 9. affect 10. others 11. than 12. the 13. if / whether 14. conscience 15. not 16. make 17. conscious 18. buying 19. that / which 20. though 21. other 22. do 23. about 24. habits 25. to

Noun Phrases with Dependent Prepositions (ii): 1-h 2-g 3- e 4- a 5- f 6-d 7-l 8-j 9-b 10-c 11-i 12-k

What makes a good Leader? 1 The 2 worth 3 gold 4 In my opinion / If you ask me 5 who / that 6 leads 7 by 8 the same 9 ability 10 Another 11 job 12 communication 13 Besides 14 attributes / qualities 15 would also 16 from 17 detail 18 Being 19 handle 20 staff 21 sleeves 22 down 23 However 24 on 25 consider

Adjectives with Dependent Prepositions (iii): 1-g 2-h 3-e 4-l 5-a 6-k 7-d 8-c 9-j 10-f 11-j 12-b

One Word, Three Uses (iii): Q1. make Q2. give Q3. put Q4. keep Q5. do Q6. give Q7. keep Q8. drive

Linking Words (ii): 1-m / 2-e / 3-n / 4-g / 5-h / 6-k / 7-a / 8-i / 9-f / 10-j / 11-c / 12-b / 13-l

Differentiating between Wants and Needs: 1) the 2) if / though 3) the more 4) he more 5) rate 6) The 7) lies 8) between 9) many

10) advertised 11) However, 12) apart from 13) few 14) life 15) off 16) appear / seem 17) reasonable / sensible 18) currently 19) faced / wrestling 20) the other 21) argument 22) least 23) giving 24) others 25) opportunity

Linking Words (iii): 1-a / 2-l / 3-g / 4-k / 5-d / 6-i / 7-j / 8-e / 9-f / 10-c / 11-h / 12-b

How Assertive Are You?

ANSWERS

1.	a-2 b-0 c-1	7.	a-2 b-0
2.	a-2 b-1 c-0	8.	a-2 b-1 c-0
3.	a-2 b-1 c-0	9.	a-1 b-2 c-0
4.	a-0 b-1 c-2	10.	a-2 b-0
5.	a-2 b-1 c-0	11.	a-2 b-1 c-0
6.	a-0 b-1 c-2	12.	a-2 b-1 c-0

WHAT YOUR SCORE MEANS

0 - 6   Join an assertiveness class where you can learn to take charge more and how to stop people exploiting you.

7 -12   You're nicely assertive and know what you want.

13-18   Don't be so pushy! Your need to be in control all the time is the result of your basic insecurity.

19-24   You're a relentless persecutor of the weak and vulnerable. In fact, you're a bit of a monster!

Giving Presentations: 1. If / When 2. golden 3. down 4. lose 5. expect 6. ensure 7. avoid 8. regarded 9. knowing 10.using 11.

every now and then / from time time 12. meaty 13. teeth 14. best 15. the other 16. preventing 17. nerves 18. practise 19. easier 20. Remains

The Environmental Impact of Packaging:
1 down 2 into 3 under 4 up 5 with 6 onto 7 about 8 on 9 of 10 in 11 in 12 to 13 with 14 for 15 before

The Rules: 1. essential or necessary 2. extra or additional 3. Defining 4. non-defining 6. written 7. WHO 8. non-defining

Phrasal Nouns (i): 1. outcry / 2. turnover / 3. output / 4. run-up / 5. showdown / 6. share-out / 7. downturn / 8. outlook / 9. outcome / 10. hold-up

Cold-Calling: 1 The 2 for 3 on 4 waste 5 Nevertheless 6 living 7 appear / seem 8 wonder 9 deal 10 the 11assure 12 exactly / precisely 13 say 14 However 15 the 16 more 17 more 18 Like 19 jobs 20 course 21 salary / wage (both possible, but with different meanings. A salary is usually paid monthly whereas a wage is paid weekly) 22 for 23 However 24 to sell 25 at all / whatsoever

Phrasal Nouns (ii): 1. comeback / 2. outbreak / 3. stand-by / 4. upkeep / 5. turn-out / 6. work-out / 7. climb-down / 8. clear-out / 9. getaway / 10. drop-outs

A Model Presentation
Matching Activity: 1-i 2-b 3-j 4-a 5-e 6-g 7-d 8-f 9-c 10-h

Sentence Order: 4 / 6 / 10 / 2 / 9 / 7 / 5 / 1 / 8 / 3

Ethical Sourcing: 1. of 2. of 3. in 4. to 5. from 6. 6. to 7. at 8. with 9. for 10. at 11. on 12. for 13. under 14. to 15. up 16. in

One Word, Three Uses (iv): Q1. strike / Q2. win / Q3. offer / Q4. make / Q5. mind / Q6. strike Q7. clear

Food Miles: 1. look 2. lines 3. the food 4.proportion 5. rest 6. grown 7. the U.K. 8. season 9. become 10. to having 11. reliance 12. awareness 13. to reduce 14. However 15. importing 16. developing 17. who 18. dependent 19. than 20. at first 21. may or might 22. appear or seem 23. bear 24. British 25. produce is

Gerund or Infinitive?

The Rules: 1. earlier 2. start 3. likes 4. general 5. particular 6. familiar 7. experiment 8. difficult 9. entail or include 10. plans 11. object 12. recommend / allow / permit / forbid

Matching Activity: 1-k 2-f 3-g 4-m 5-i 6-l 7-n 8-a 9-b 10-e 11-d 12-b 13-j 14-h

One Word, Three Uses (v): Q1. come Q2. be Q3. make Q4. do Q5. draw Q6. put

Pet Hates: 1. of 2. crazy 3. persuade 4. The 5. people 6. having 7. a law was introduced 8. the 9. of returning 10. to do 11. to 12. practice 13. the 14. appear / seem 15. worse 16. getting 17. Moreover, 18. which 19. wonder 20. literate 21. I say 22. good old 23. private 24. use 25. public

TO + ING: 1-m/2-h/3-j/4-a/5-i/6-k/7-b/8-d/9-f/10-e/11-g/12-c/13-l

Phrasal Adjectives: 1. get-out / 2. fallback / 3. takeover / 4. cutoff / 5. grown-up / 6. runaway / 7. knock-out / 8. takeaway / 9. giveaway / 10. pay-out

BOOKS

O is a symbol of the world, of oneness and unity. In different cultures it also means the "eye," symbolizing knowledge and insight. We aim to publish books that are accessible, constructive and that challenge accepted opinion, both that of academia and the "moral majority."

Our books are available in all good English language bookstores worldwide. If you don't see the book on the shelves ask the bookstore to order it for you, quoting the ISBN number and title. Alternatively you can order online (all major online retail sites carry our titles) or contact the distributor in the relevant country, listed on the copyright page.

See our website www.o-books.net for a full list of over 500 titles, growing by 100 a year.

And tune in to myspiritradio.com for our book review radio show, hosted by June-Elleni Laine, where you can listen to the authors discussing their books.

MySpiritRadio